# ABC TO MINISTRY

## Applying Biblical Concepts to Ministry

SHARON C. LENIOR

Scribes By God

# MOMENTS OF IMPACT

There are a few people that I specifically want to acknowledge for very particular reasons. LaTanyia Craig, though you are not my granny by blood, God showed me there was no difference when he allowed you to take a seat in my heart. It was you that God used to deliver the message that his Word is not complicated, people are. The conversation that we had sitting around the table that day at the church changed my thoughts forever on ministry and how it is done. This new insight launched me into writing my first book, so thank you for trusting me with what God put on your heart to share. That moment and your words that day, will forever change me and impact my ministry for the better. Love you, Granny.

# MOMENTS OF IMPACT

There are many people who have spoken great words, some simple and some complicated, but not always impactful. One day I had a friend offer to unexpectedly help me with an idea I had. I was surprised. I didn't understand why he was willing to help me without any guarantees of the outcome. It was at that moment, he said something that was so matter-of-fact, but it stuck with me. God allowed that phrase to take on it's own purpose in my life until this day, and I have never looked at helping people the same way since.

**"Everyone needs a little help sometimes.
It only takes one person to do a little bit more to change someone else's life forever."**

-Matthew Ryan Dunbar

I have written this book believing that as God has assigned me to do a little bit more in simplifying the dynamics and order of ministry, that the breakdown and details of this book will change someone's perception or life, as both of you have changed mine.

God Bless You, Both.

# ACKNOWLEDGEMENTS

I would like to thank my foundation, my family, Tasha Butcher, Victoria and Taron Epps, Jasmine Jett and Zinna Butcher. Thank you all for supporting me, my ministry, my dreams, this book and all that is to come. As we continue to follow the voice of God in our endeavors, I pray that God continues to download new ideas, visions and goals into your new seasons. This is just the beginning.

To my parents, Bishop Dietrich Butcher and Evangelist Hazel Butcher, thank you for being the example of godly parents and leadership. I couldn't have made it to this point without your lifetime of guidance, wisdom and prayers that have covered me through my storms. I am truly thankful for the mantles in which you both carry. The lessons learned, the lessons taught and the lessons that are coming. Thank you for your persistence in raising us in a household filled with God's presence.

Thank you, Bishop Charles and Elect Lady Patty Sawyer of Sanctuary of Prayer, in Valdosta, GA. You have been my second set of parents naturally and spiritually all my life. Your decades of friendship with my family have allowed my siblings and I to always be surrounded with love, guidance, truth and sound doctrine outside of our home. Thank you for always taking my calls, praying and leading me as God sees fit. Your example of God driven friendship and leadership has left an imprint in my heart that I can never fully put into words but I am forever grateful.

I would also like to thank Bishop R.W. Freeman and his wife, Evangelist Elisa Freeman for giving me your unwavering feedback and direction on the content of this book. Your feedback and grounded insight helped me complete this assignment with a level of excellence. Words cannot express my gratitude.

**Though all others may have been acknowledged, all glory belongs to God.**

It is through his grace and mercy, his love and kindness, his Word and his voice, that I am able to find the right words to complete the assignment at hand.

**To God be all the glory.**

"Because one person disobeyed God, Many became sinners. But because one other person obeyed God, many will be made righteous."

-Romans 5:19 NLT

# TABLE OF CONTENTS

Introduction ................................................................2

Chapter 1: Come As You Are .................................4

Chapter 2: What Must I Do to Be Saved? .............11

Chapter 3: Is That All to It?.................................13

Chapter 4: What Does God Say About Serving?.......16

Chapter 5: How a Leader Should Govern................20

Chapter 6: The Characteristics of a Shepherd (Pastor).......26

Chapter 7: Choosing Good Ground .......................30

Chapter 8: The Inner Workings of the Church ........35

Chapter 9: Praise & Worship................................38

Chapter 10: Knowledge is Power...........................40

Chapter 11: To Church or Not to Church?..............48

Chapter 12: What is a Five-Fold Ministry? .............50

Chapter 13: The Call vs. The Ministry....................53

Chapter 14: The Face of a Christian & The Heart of God.......58

Chapter 15: Symptoms of Spiritual Sickness .........64

Chapter 16: Right Place, Wrong Time ...................67

Chapter 17: Obedience vs. Manipulation................75

Chapter 18: Money vs. Offering.............................83

Chapter 19: Is Tithing a Requirement? ..................87

Chapter 20: Choosing Between Offering or Tithes .......95

Chapter 21: Should Pastors Receive a Salary............97

Chapter 22: Restoring Honor to the House Of God.........103

Declaration Page........................................... 104

# Note from the Author

In my writing you will notice that the names used for the devil are not capitalized. This intentional choice reflects my belief that the devil does not hold enough significance to warrant the respect and recognition that capitalization implies. By not capitalizing the devil's name, I aim to diminish his importance and emphasize the power and supremacy of God. This decision aligns with my belief that despite who, what, when, where and how the devil attempts to attack, that he will never be more than God's footstool and adversary to the Kingdom of God. I choose to focus on the victories past, present and future and stand in confidence that God will always be the one & only true living God.

Thank you for joining me on this journey.

# Introduction

## I Timothy 3:14-15 ESV

*"I hope to come to you soon, but I am writing these things to you so that, if I delay, you may know how one ought to behave in the household of God, which is the church of the living God, a pillar and buttress of the truth."*

The subjects and information discussed in this book are not written by chance. Each chapter has been written with the guidance of the Holy Spirit, so young and old alike may receive clarity in the most simplistic way.

In my obedience to God, I speak over every person who will read, encounter, refer or gift this book. May everyone that God has intended for this book to impact receive a simplistic understanding of ministry and honor in the House of God. May their hearts be open for understanding. Let not offense nor defense hijack this opportunity for growth and spiritual stability. God, we pray this book ignites and re-ignites a burning desire to be pleasing unto you. Let the impact of this book be an everlasting one, founded on your Word so that your house can be honored as you have intended. May the words in this book be received in love for the glory of your Kingdom. Amen.

Last year, God laid heavily on my heart to speak on the foundations of honoring the House of God. There have been so many compromises in today's churches that many have adopted an identity to be politically correct, displaying a worldly demeanor. True places of worship and sound doctrine have become a little more difficult to find, though there are still authentic churches that represent God without compromise. Churches will have to account for the practices in which they operate. Time is running out. God is requiring his people to bring the honor back to his house before judgment is rendered. The time is now.

## I Peter 4:17 ESV

*"For it is time for judgment to begin at the household of God; and if it begins with us, what will be the outcome for those who do not obey the gospel of God"*

Let's dive in.

# Chapter 1

## Come As You Are

How do you represent God? As the Bible tells us how we should conduct ourselves, the Bible also addresses how we should dress. The Word states that women should dress themselves in modest apparel and that beauty should come from within. We should reflect a gentle spirit. Though the Word does not state directly how men should dress, it does state that men should not dress in women's garments.

### I Timothy 2:9-10 NLT

*"And I want women to be modest in their appearance. They should wear decent and appropriate clothing and not draw attention to themselves by the way they fix their hair or by wearing gold or pearls or expensive clothes. For women who claim to be devoted to God should make themselves attractive by the good things they do."*

### I Peter 3:2-5 ESV

*...when they see your respectful and pure conduct. Do not let your adorning be external-the braiding of hair and the putting on of gold jewelry, or the clothing you wear-but let your adorning be the hidden person of the heart with the imperishable beauty of a gentle and quiet spirit, which in God's sight is very precious. For this is how the holy women who hoped in God used to adorn themselves by submitting to their own husbands.*

# Deuteronomy 22:5 NLT

*"A woman must not put on men's clothing, and a man must not wear women's clothing. Anyone who does this is detestable in the sight of the Lord your God."*

Then, there is "come as you are." Does this mean anything goes in the Kingdom? Absolutely, not. The term, "come as you are" has been quoted so much from generation to generation and church to church, that most people have no idea where it actually came from. This is often a term that is misrepresented and manipulated to justify wearing any and everything in the House of God. You might be surprised to know that "come as you are" is just a depiction of scripture and not an actual scripture at all. Though there are plenty of times that Jesus called us to come to him in scripture, it was never in those exact words, but it does not change the heart of his invitation. God tells us in scripture that we are to come to him in whatever state we are in and let him work out what is wrong within us or around us. Though the term "come as you are" is the right idea, it has often been manipulated for self-gratification and justifying one's actions in situations that requires people to be mindful and use wisdom in their choices. God encourages people who thirst for God to come to him, even without money. His Word is free and fulfilling and comes without pre-requisites.

# Isaiah 55:1-3 ESV

*"Come, everyone who thirst, come to the waters; and he who has no money, come, buy and eat! Come, buy wine and milk without money and without price. Why do you spend your money for that which is not bread, and your labor for that which does not satisfy? Listen diligently to me, and eat what is good, and delight yourselves in rich food. Incline your ear, and come to me; hear, that you soul may live; and I will make with you an everlasting covenant, my steadfast, sure love for David."*

# Isaiah 1:18 ESV

*"Come now, let us reason together, says the Lord: though your sins are like scarlet, they shall be as white as snow; though they are red like crimson, they shall become like wool."*

# Mark 10:13-16 NLT

*"One day some parents brought their children to Jesus so he could touch and bless them. But the disciples scolded the parents for bothering him. When Jesus saw what was happening, he was angry with his disciples. He said to them, 'Let the children come to me. Don't stop them! For the Kingdom of God belongs to those who are like these children. I tell you the truth, anyone who doesn't receive the Kingdom of God like a child will never enter it.' Then he took the children in his arms and placed his hands on their heads and blessed them."*

# Matthew 11:28 NLT

*"Then Jesus said, 'Come to me, all of you who are weary and carry heavy burdens, and I will give you rest."*

"Come as you are," is a statement to express not allowing anything to stop you from coming to the House of God. We are not required to be perfect to come to God. Our only requirement is to be willing to do what it takes to be changed. God will do the rest. This understanding is usually tainted with the world's unrealistic expectations that those who are saved or in church should not have any faults. Those who believe that, often do not understand the concept that the church operates as a spiritual hospital. You may have no desire to go to church but something as simple as showing up to see your grandbaby's part in the Resurrection play can be all that it takes. Just being there puts you in position for God to deal with you. Someone could tell a testimony of how God helped them get out of something they're in right now. God has many ways to deal with us, and we do not have to be perfect for him to do so. Many people think that they are too far gone or do not think they are worthy enough to step inside a church. Here's the secret, none of us are worthy enough, but God shows us grace and allows us to experience him for ourselves. What people wear in the church and how the church manages it, is one of the struggles. It is one of the biggest turnoffs for people who have felt judged for their appearance in the church when handled incorrectly. Those who are unaware or struggle with what they should not wear in ministry should not include members of leadership. Leaders should be held to a higher standard because they should be the example of what godly women and men look like. Leadership should be mindful of whether those who are not dressed accordingly are members, new Christians, guests or frequent attendees.

So, what is the standard of how one should dress in church? Simply put, modest and appropriate. With all the different types of people that you will encounter in church, each person has a unique relationship with God. As people find their way to church, you will find people at various levels of their walk with God. This is something you will always need to consider. You cannot hold the same expectation of those who are not saved to the same expectation of a new or seasoned Christian. Some attendees may not have a relationship at all with Christ. Wisdom must play a part in how leaders handle the congregation. While every church should have open doors regardless of one's spiritual state, there must be a reverence and standard that we uphold in ministry. These things can be done discreetly in church to avoid drawing attention to someone's apparel. Though there is a certain standard in the House of God, remember that God influences the change, not us. This is something we cannot force. For example, if a visiting young lady is wearing a short dress that is revealing, it may not be wise to sit her at the front of the church where her attire may be a distraction. The way she sits down, crosses her legs, or even how she bounces or sways to the worship music can all unknowingly play a part in a distraction. People who dress this way may not have a negative agenda and we must keep in mind that their short dress may be the best choice from their closet. This could very well be their best attempt to look appropriate. Some people who have not grown up in the church may not know or may have a distorted understanding of what's appropriate in church. We want to be sure that they have ample time to build a relationship with God. This does not mean that the church should abandon their standards or compromise our integrity for more attendees. Some churches have compromised their integrity for more members and worldly acceptance. This makes it difficult for new attendees or those new to Christ to witness the acceptable christian behavior and attire by seeing seasoned saints properly dressed. Churches never operate looking for acceptance from anyone but God.

Churches should operate in such a way that people should want to know what they must do to be accepted into the Kingdom. The more that people get that into their spirit, the less likely they will be offended about receiving godly correction. Another way to deal with someone's clothes being too short is to hand them a lap cloth as you seat them. This can be a common practice for ushers any time someone wears a dress above their knees or for all females who sit in the front or the first and last seat in each row. This will take the attention off any one person. This approach can still cause a lot of angry responses, but it is necessary to do what is needed to maintain dignity in the House of God. If you seat a woman wearing a too short dress a couple of rows back and toward the middle of the rows and not at the end of the row, following up with a cloth may not always be needed. This can be a very delicate situation. If a Pastor allows for other leaders to act on their behalf, it would be best to pick someone who is tactful with their words, has discernment and can filter through all the scenarios that will determine how to proceed with someone. Be mindful about where you sit them and who is also in that row.

You may not have the perfect seating, but all these strategies may help. Try to avoid placing them in the back row, as this may make them feel ostracized or judged. Leaders should not sit someone dressed provocatively in the front row or next to someone with a wandering eye or lust issues. You do not need to know everyone's business but between discernment, good leadership and what you are aware of, you should have some good guidelines. Every ministry team should have leaders with discernment, wisdom and the ability to hear God clearly to handle their assigned ministry wisely. Leaders placed in the position to make godly corrections must have a heart for people or you will end up with a ministry of bullies and judgmental people; which is the last thing you want. Does this mean that we handle each person the same? No. Some people come to seek God.

Everything we do should be done in a godly way and in love. Seeing Sister Shake and Bake come to church with tight clothes on, legs out and switching hard does not give you permission to be nasty toward her or talk to her disrespectfully. Some people need more time in God's presence before there is a noticeable change. Our timing is not God's timing. Meantime, we should do our part in love. Sometimes, what people battle in their spiritual life can visibly be seen by what they wear, say or do. We should be concerned with their spirit before we're concerned with their flesh.

As leaders, you must recognize where people are in their spiritual walk with God. Show them the love of Christ and let God change their hearts. You are more likely to witness the Holy Spirit at work when you stop trying to do God's job. God will change their hearts before you could ever change their minds. Healthy decisions are more likely to take place when people make decisions based on their relationship with God, in his timing, rather than someone else's. We want to create an atmosphere for true Christians who have a heart for God and not a church full of people who just look the part. With patience, love and true teachings of the Word, you may start to witness subtle changes as people encounter the Holy Spirit more. Their apparel may be the last thing you see change. Just prepare to be patient. Someone coming to church doesn't mean they're ready to change. They may attend service out of habit, curiosity and some out of a desire to do something different. Most people will watch their surroundings before they commit to getting involved; so be the Godly example and not the judge. So, when do you speak up and have a conversation with them about the way they are dressed? Well, guess what? There is a scripture for that also.

## Ephesians 2:19-22 NKJV

*Now therefore, you are no longer strangers and foreigners, but fellow citizens with the saints and members of the household of God, having been built on the foundation of the apostles and prophets, Jesus Christ Himself being the chief cornerstone, in whom the whole building, being fitted together, grows into a holy temple in the Lord, in whom you also are being built together for a dwelling place of God in the Spirit.*

Once that person is no longer a stranger in the House of God, meaning once they have become consistent and built some relationships within the church and with God; there should be enough foundation and growth to allow some corrections. Timing in this case is vital to doing this correctly. This should not be decided by anyone but the Pastor unless given authorization to make this decision. What you think and feel about someone's attire is irrelevant if your Pastor does not release you to say anything. Some members may have the right intention but are unable to use tact or compassion. The approach and timing of a correction can determine if the correction is received in love or offense. Someone who is seasoned in God and the church, should not require as long of a grace period to see change, than new Christians; especially if they're leaders. Leaders should be an example. The church cannot be so concerned with offending people that we are okay with offending God by allowing any and everything within God's House. We must not compromise the Word of God for temporary acceptance. Who do you serve? Remember, the world is supposed to be offended, because dark and light cannot exist together. However, we should attempt to not offend anyone well within the realm of still being obedient to the Word of God. God says that offenses will come but warns those who offend intentionally.

## Matthew 18:7 NKJV

*"Woe to the world because of offenses! For offenses must come, but woe to that man by whom the offense comes!..."*

<u>Take a moment to repeat this prayer:</u>
God, I pray for wisdom in all that I do. So that I may move according to your will, to the sound of your voice and in the presence of the Holy Spirit. Let me represent you in my approach to others so that I might show them grace, the way you have shown grace to me. Let me not operate in anger, prejudice or judgment. Let my words and my conduct be honorable to you, as I pray that they see you in me, in all that I do. In your name, I pray. Amen.

# Chapter 2

## What Must I Do to Be Saved?

### Matthew 16:24 ESV

*"Then Jesus told his disciples, 'If anyone would come after me, let him deny himself and take up his cross and follow me."*

If you desire a relationship with Jesus, deny living for yourself by allowing God to be the one you choose to follow. Recognizing when you get it wrong is humbling. This is a lesson I learned in my spiritual journey. Sometimes, I would do what I wanted to do and then expected God to follow behind me in my decisions, just in case I needed him. Whenever an emergency would happen, I would call on God and expect him to fix the outcome of my decision. I had spiritually taken on the damsel in distress syndrome without realizing it. My ideology was not to let God make the decisions and follow him, it was to act on my plans and expect God to follow me. I wasn't allowing God to be my decision-maker. I treated God like an emergency button when things didn't go as I had hoped. When you decide that you want to live for God, you must understand there is no more "I" in your decisions. You must let God go before you and then be willing to follow him, not the other way around.

### Romans 10:9-10 ESV

*"Because, if you confess with your mouth that Jesus is Lord and believe in your heart that God raised him from the dead, you will be saved. For with the heart, one believes and is justified, and with the mouth one confesses and is saved."*

What must you do to be saved, is a question that some believers and churches can complicate but it is quite simple. There are three simple steps to be saved. Believe that Jesus died for our sins, God raised him from the dead and confess it with your mouth. That is all that it takes to be saved. Going to church, being a good person or doing community service is not enough to get you into Heaven. Never exclude God from the equation. Without God, there is only an eternity of fire awaiting you.

## Ephesians 2:8-9 ESV

*"For by grace you have been saved through faith. And this is not your own doing; it is the gift of God, not a result of works, so that no one may boast."*

It is not through our own actions that we are qualified to be saved. As Ephesians states, it is not a result of our own doing but one of God's.

## John 1:12 ESV

*"But to all who did receive him, who believed in his name, he gave the right to become Children of God"*

Everyone will have an opportunity to be saved but not everyone will accept the invitation. God only gives the right to become a Child of God to those who accepted him and believe in his name.

# Chapter 3

## Is That All to It?

Is that all that is needed? Yes. The word is very black and white and sometimes red, depending on what version of the Bible you are reading. But seriously though, yes, that is all you must do to be saved, but it is not all that you have to do to stay saved. Let me explain.

The Bible is full of guidance through stories that allow us to put his direction and instructions into context. While getting saved requires nothing more than truth, belief and a confession that God gave his only son to die for our sins; we must strive to obey God by living according to his Word. Let me give an obvious example. Someone can become a Christian and then sin. Confessing that Jesus died for their sins does not exclude them from future sins committed. Any sin we commit after Jesus died on the cross requires us to be accountable for our sins, repent out of our mouths and request forgiveness. God knows our intentions. He always sees our heart in everything we do, good or bad.

There are false narratives that linger as truth but can cost you your place in Heaven. Some people believe that if you are a good person who does honorable deeds, it'll get you through Heaven's doors. Good deeds are not equivalent to salvation. Salvation is the only thing that can get you through the big pearly gates. We must repent and mean it with the intention to not offend God again. True repentance is reflected by the desire to not disappoint or go against God intentionally or in the same way we had in our past. There should be a lesson in acknowledging what we have done that has dishonored God.

It's no different than being in a relationship with someone and hurting them. When you apologize, you usually express how unintentional it was and seek forgiveness. If you hurt them again, your intention becomes questionable. The current apology does not excuse all future behavior. There is a requirement to get back in that person's good grace if they are willing to give you another chance. God requires the same commitment. We can fail God, but because of who God is and his grace and mercy, he allows us to seek forgiveness over and over again. The apology must come from an honest and repented heart. Because God knows our heart, he also knows our intention. Repentance that does not come with a real desire to change or the intention to not make the same mistake again is not true repentance. Falling again does not mean that there was not a heart to repent. People can make the same mistake more than once even if they really want to do better. It is the desire to really change and the actions behind it that determines if there is true repentance. In order for you to get complete clarity, there is something you must understand. Because we are born in sin, our flesh is addicted to sin. As Christians, our spirit is drawn to God, the anointing, his glory and his works. Our flesh will crave the desire to do the wrong thing or things that are not biblical. This is why the Word tells us to keep our flesh under submission. To do so we must be able to control our flesh with our spirit. Our flesh will crave to sin again, but we can control our flesh through consistently reading his Word and prayer and fasting. This allows our spirit to dominate our flesh, lessening our craving for sinful behavior.

In a relationship context, if you are not sorry for what you have done, there is no true repentance. Though you may have fooled people around you, God will always know what's in your heart. You can never fool God. Your apology can only be as good as your honesty. This usually requires a change in behavior and eliminating some people or things that may jeopardize your relationship. This works the same way in a relationship with God. Being saved is not just something you do. It's a commitment. Being saved is an agreement of submission, an acknowledgment of sacrifice and a willingness to spread the good news of God to bring others to Christ. You must be willing to be a vessel for God, which allows him to use you for his glory without limitations. This cannot be done if you dwell in darkness. God (light) and the devil (darkness) cannot co-exist in the same vessel.

# I John 1:6 ESV

*"If we say we have fellowship with him while we walk in darkness, we lie and do not practice the truth."*

# Chapter 4

## What Does God Say About Serving?

If I have not lost you as a friend throughout this book already, this chapter is not the subject that is going to make you all warm and fuzzy inside. It may even be a little hard to swallow, so get your magnifying glass out because the details are in the fine print. Can you serve in ministry if you are unsaved or compromised as a Christian? A Christian who is compromised is someone who has chosen to be partially obedient to the Word of God. Partial obedience is complete disobedience. A compromised state causes people to pick and choose certain parts of the Bible they have chosen to follow. Compromised Christians are not easy to identify but tend to hide or keep secrets about their life that do not line up with God. Compromising your salvation only opens doors for other things, like lying, guilt, shame and sin itself. Compromising the Word will always be a failed attempt to negotiate what God has already written. His Word is never changing. A person who declares they are saved and not married but is still having sex or shacking up with someone is an example of a compromised Christian. So how is shacking up a compromise? We, as Christians, are to be an example of godly living. The Word says we are to strive to be more like Christ. There is no scripture that God approves of us shacking up (living) with someone we are not married to. However, there is scripture that speaks of avoiding temptation because the flesh is weak, though our spirit is willing to do what is right. This is where shacking up becomes a problem. God is not looking for perfection, he is looking for obedience. Once you know it is wrong, you are knowingly operating out of the will of God. This scripture tells us that we should not put ourselves in a situation that will be a temptation to our flesh. We must watch for opportunities that the enemy may present to us that can bait us to be tempted.

## Matthew 26:41 KJV

*"Watch and pray, that ye enter not into temptation: the spirit indeed is willing, but the flesh is weak."*

Many people try to separate being saved from their personal life. If you are one of those people, you are spiritually in an unhealthy place. This type of separation will often cause you to live a lifestyle that contradicts the Word of God. People tend to make going to church part of their routine. They take on the mindset that going to church is a lifestyle, but it's salvation that is the lifestyle. What you do in church does not determine how much you love God. God says that following him is proof that you love him. We must not come up with our own ideology on how to love God, especially if he has made it clear that his love language is obedience.

## John 14:15 NLT

*"If you love me, obey my commandments."*

So, what about serving as an unbeliever? Can an unbeliever serve in ministry though they are not saved? I promise to give you all the clarity you need so that you don't close this book still wondering about the answer to these difficult questions.

There are many things in the church that need managing every time the doors of the church open. Unbelievers who are members of the church can serve but it all depends on where. Certain ministries are built to help usher in the Holy Spirit, which means to set an atmosphere where we invite God in to have an encounter. This is where praise and worship and prayer come in. These ministries should consist of people who are saved and living an un-compromised life. Someone who has not accepted Jesus as their Lord and Savior should not be working in these ministries. It does not matter if the unbeliever has a beautiful voice or if they are good at what they do. Serving God in these positions require you to operate in spirit to usher in the presence of God; not just any spirit but the Holy Spirit. This is the responsibility of the Pastor to uphold this biblical standard.

## John 4:24 NLT

*"For God is Spirit, so those who worship him must worship in spirit and in truth."*

John 4:24 emphasizes that we must be in spirit to worship God because he is Spirit. To honor God in praise and worship or prayer, you must be a willing vessel. You must be willing to let God use you how he sees fit. If you are unsaved, you have already denied God the ability to use you in this area. You may be participating in the songs and enjoying the presence of the Holy Spirit, but an unclean spirit can not lead in this manner. In the state of being unsaved, you have already denied his invitation to forgive you of all your sins and accept salvation.

## II Timothy 2:21 ESV

*"Therefore, if anyone cleanses himself from what is dishonorable, he will be a vessel for honorable use, set apart as holy, useful to the master of the house, ready for every good work."*

To be useful in God's House, we must be set apart as holy and be a vessel for honorable use. We can only be a vessel for honorable use if we have repented from our sins and changed our lives to live for God. To be set apart is to not look, act, talk or think like we use to without Christ. Now look at that scripture in a different interpretation.

## II Timothy 2:21 NLT

*"Work hard so you can present yourself to God and receive his approval. Be a good worker, one who does not need to be ashamed and who correctly explains the word of truth."*

If a man or woman of God has compromised their salvation, they cannot present themselves to God as one approved. If someone is an unbeliever, they cannot be at their best. We can only be at our best if God dwells within us. We cannot offer ourselves to God as a vessel to be used in ministry, while simultaneously denying our heart to God in full. II Corinthians 6:14-15 is often referred to in relationships, but is also valid in ministry.

## II Corinthians 6:14-15 NLT

*Don't team up with those who are unbelievers. How can righteousness be a partner with wickedness? How can light live with darkness? What harmony can there be between Christ and the devil? How can a believer be a partner with an unbeliever?*

It's not the approval of the church that makes you unfit to serve God if you are compromised and an unbeliever. It is God himself. The Word says that you must do your best to present yourself as one approved to serve as an honorable vessel. I am sure you have witnessed someone who is not saved working in the church. However, there is a distinction between serving God and serving in the House of God. Unbelievers and compromised Christians cannot be honorable vessels according to scripture, but they can still pursue a relationship with God. Pursuing a relationship with God is always possible until your last breath.

When serving in ministry, you are ministering to the people of God. It requires you to know first-hand who God is and have a personal relationship with him. However, compromised Christians and unbelievers may serve in certain areas of the House of God. An appropriate way for them to serve is volunteering to help clean up the church, working security or parking details. In a nutshell, God see's people who are saved and not compromised, fit to serve in ministry, and are set apart, holy and ready for all good work. This should be the standard for ministry. People who are unsaved and compromised should not be permitted to serve in ministry but can put their hands to work in the church.

# Chapter 5

## How a Leader Should Govern

Throughout the Word of God, there is a clear understanding on how a leader should govern themselves, in and out of the church and in their personal life. This chapter highlights a few key traits every Christian should incorporate to fulfill the character God calls us to embrace.

### Titus 1:7-8 NLT

*"A church leader is a manager of God's household, so he must live a blameless life. He must not be arrogant or quick-tempered; he must not be a heavy drinker, violent, or dishonest with money. Rather, he must enjoy having guests in his home, and he must love what is good. He must live wisely and be just. He must live a devout and disciplined life."*

## 1. Exercise oversight not under compulsion

Compulsion is a natural reaction, not a spiritual one. Compulsively responding to things does not give you enough time to process things naturally or spiritually. This is equivalent to impulse shopping. When you are in the store buying everything you wrote on your shopping list, you have a sense of control over your time and budget. Compulsive responses deprive you from making efficient and wise decisions. It will also cause you to make decisions based on things that should not have an impact at all. This is how impulse buying at the register impacts your shopping. You will end up buying things that are not needed for the task at hand, requiring more effort, work, attention, money or more energy than necessary. It is usually accompanied by a bit of regret, like thinking, "I really should not have bought that, spent that or I didn't need that."

Compulsive reactions are a sign that there is a lack of self-discipline. A godly woman or man with no self-discipline is a red flag in their spiritual walk. Striving to live without sin can only be possible if we think about our decisions before making them and daily repentance. The enemy will always continue to tempt you; he tempted the Lord Jesus. Without discipline, we leave the door wide open for the enemy to suck us into an ungodly behavior. This can reflect poorly on a Man or Woman of God, the ministry, and the church. We cannot carry the character of a respectable Christian if we are unable to control our impulses. Without godly control, our flesh becomes our primary decision-maker. It is our spiritual responsibility to call our flesh into submission. To have godly self-control is to not only think before acting, but to think of how to react to things in a way that still honors God. This should not taint who we are in God or the reputation of those who serve God. Your obligation as a Man or Woman of God is not just a representation of you, but the representation of those in the body of Christ and most importantly, the representation of God himself.

1. Based on how you behave and live your life, who do you say God is?
2. Do you respond to people impulsively or take the time to think about what you are going to say?
3. Do you think about how your words impact others?
4. Does your words give life or death to the situation?
5. Explain why you do or don't.
6. From 1-10, how do you rate yourself on how well you respond to other people or things that disrupt your spirit? (1 being impulsive and 10 being calm and self-controlled. Circle one).

1 2 3 4 5 6 7 8 9 10

5. What area do you think you can improve in and how?

There are so many people that claim to be Christians and have no spiritual understanding. Many people know about Christ, but do not know him personally. The Word says to know him is to follow him.

## I John 2:4 NASB

*"The one who says, 'I have come to know Him,' and does not keep His commandments, is a liar, and the truth is not in him."*

You cannot have a relationship with Christ if you are not pursuing God by reading his Word, praying, and living for Christ. It would be like marrying someone that you refuse to take the time to get to know and then brag about how great they are. Have you ever heard someone frustrated with the fact that someone has a lot to say about them? Their response is, "They don't even know me." That is exactly Jesus' position. God's posture is equivalent to saying do not pretend to know me when you have done nothing to cultivate (build) a relationship with me. Jesus says if you deny him, then he will deny you. Do not claim Jesus in secret, but not in front of those you encounter. This is the only way that Jesus will claim you in front of His Father.

## Matthew 10:32-33 KJV

*Whosoever therefore shall confess me before men, him will I confess also before my Father which is in heaven. But whosoever shall deny me before men, him will I also deny before my Father which is in heaven.*

If we are men and women of God, our behavior should reflect Christ. Responding impulsively allows flesh to make the first decision. This is a dangerous practice because denying Christ can also be done without ever opening your mouth. Our actions can also deny Christ when they are not honorable or do not represent God, which is why it is vital for Christians to think before we move. The time that it takes to think before we act, is the time that your spirit should be getting your flesh into submission. If you are saved and operating in the spirit, you are relying on God and not yourself to take the lead. Allowing this to be your mindset every day denies the enemy access to the forefront of your life. The moment you allow negative impulses to dictate your behavior; you have denied Christ from taking the lead. Giving the enemy first access not only gives the devil priority over God but can damage the reputation of who you are in Christ. Getting your flesh under submission is not always the easiest thing to do. Being self-disciplined, learning self-discipline and having no discipline speaks highly to where you are spiritually. Impulsiveness is a sign of spiritual immaturity.

## 2. Not lording it over those allotted to your charge, but proving to be examples to the flock

To lord over someone is to hover over people, to micromanage them. If God has assigned you to lead, scripture says not to micromanage or hover over those assigned to you. If you feel the need to micromanage the people under you, this says more about your leadership than your congregation. Either you have not effectively been able to teach those assigned to you or you have a control issue. God gives us free reign to make decisions for ourselves. This is why we have the right to decide whether we want to accept Jesus into our hearts or not. If this option is given by God, then who are we to require more from others than God requires from us? God does not give us an option to choose him just to then give us leadership that will micromanage our lives. If you are a micromanager, you must ask yourself two questions, can I effectively lead and are they my assignment? If either of those are no, then seek God for clarity or how you can become more efficient in your leadership style. Sometimes it is a matter of waiting for the correct timing for a teaching moment. You never want to teach a child how to do a math problem while they are climbing on the monkey bars outside. Environment and timing can impact the ability to teach effectively and learn and retain the information being given. Use wisdom in your choices, relying on God to tell you who, what, when, where and why.

If we ask God, we cannot go wrong, but if we don't wait for the answer from God, asking becomes ineffective. Be patient.

## 3. You younger men, likewise, be subject to your elders

Age is not a solo reason for placement in ministry but regardless of your knowledge, the Word says to be subject to your elders. Always be in a position to respect your elders and forever be a student. Regardless of whether you become a teacher, you should always have the heart of a student, willing with eagerness to learn. Their experience can offer some insight that you may prevent you from having to experience things yourself. Always show respect for those God has graced to live on this Earth before you were ever conceived.

## 4. All of you clothe yourselves with humility toward one another, for God is opposed to the proud, but gives grace to the humble

Humility takes confidence in knowing who you are. You are to remain humble and not become boastful. Never take an approach that you are better than or further along than someone else. God does not smile down on those who think more of themselves than they are. No matter how anointed we believe we are or how far along in the ministry we have come, we have all fallen short. In the Kingdom of God, there is no such thing as being better than anyone else, though you may be held to a higher standard. There is such a thing as being more anointed than someone else, but even then, the anointing is not ours to brag about, because it is God's; we just operate in it. Sometimes, pride can be a position that we pick up without realizing it. There have and will always be someone proud and prideful about how much knowledge they have about the Word of God. It can be very honorable to have that much knowledge, but those type of people must be intentional about staying humble. People who have fallen victim to the enemies' tactics can sometimes look down on someone who is learning the Word or asking questions.

What may seem obvious to them but not to others can build inappropriate confidence that they may not recognize as pride or boasting. They can become offended that someone disagrees with their interpretation of scripture or feel they are more qualified for a position than someone else. This can often lead to a bitter heart or change of heart posture. This is a prime example of how the enemy will pervert something that should have been a blessing. This person would be great at being able to teach others, but someone with this issue can be damaging to a ministry if positioned before they correct this problem. This type of person knows better. They will usually not admit out loud when they are wrong or will refuse correction because of lack of respect for who gives the correction or have a sense of superiority. This is usually driven by their own prideful posture. Regardless of the title and position you hold in ministry; you should never stop being a student. You can never learn everything.

## I Corinthians 4:7 NKJV

*"For who makes you differ from another? And what do you have that you did not receive? Now if you did indeed receive it, why do you boast as if you had not received it?"*

We must be careful not to get ahead of ourselves and become full of pride and ego. There have been some great women and men of God who have fallen due to their heart posture. Pride and ego can easily slip through the cracks. When your heart posture goes unchecked, it can cause pride to be the fastest growing seed in your life. Heart posture is the intention of the heart. Without an intentional desire to be more like Christ, our emotions can easily start to dictate our behavior. Anything we do in the name of God should be done with love, respect, and humbleness. Once you become full of pride, feel untouchable, overly relevant or entitled, you are no longer representing God according to the Word. You are operating in a place of self, which is not pleasing to God. No matter how much you try to hide it, your heart posture will eventually become evident in your actions. What is done in the dark will always come to light, whether it manifests physically or spiritually.

# Chapter 6

## The Characteristics of a Shepherd (Pastor)

### I Timothy 3:1-7 NLT

*"This is a trustworthy saying: 'If someone aspires to be a church leader, he desires an honorable position.' So, a church leader must be a man whose life is above approach. He must be faithful to his wife. He must exercise self-control, live wisely, and have a good reputation. He must enjoy having guests in his home, and he must be able to teach. He must not be a heavy drinker or be violent. He must be gentle, not quarrelsome, and not love money. He must manage his own family well, having children who respect and obey him. For if a man cannot manage his own household, how can he take care of God's church? A church leader must not be a new believer, because he might become proud, and the devil would cause him to fall. Also, people outside the church must speak well of him so that he will not be disgraced and fall into the devil's trap."*

The Bible speaks on what qualities your Pastor must have to be in good standing as a leader in the Kingdom to effectively be used by God. I Timothy 3:1-7 is just one scripture that lays out some key things to uphold as a standard. We are not to become judgmental as if the Pastor is not human and prone to make mistakes. However, the number one sign that should not be ignored is consistency in their shortcoming. For example, a pastor who is not self-controlled and has a blowup may not show himself in the best light, but he is human. Once the pastor acknowledges it, repents and thrives going forward without further incident, it is safe to say that he made a mistake and has done what is biblically required of him. We cannot assume at any point in time that behind closed doors the Pastor has not already asked for forgiveness, so be cautious when making a judgment call. If this same pastor, has a reputation of having blow ups, throwing things, cheating, yelling, lying etc., this is when you need to get before God and have a deeper conversation. It's not just physical or visible acts, but acts that are continued without true repentance of the heart.

For an example, a Pastor who may have cheated on his wife, according to the Word of God can still be redeemed. One who is a repetitive cheater and has repeatedly asked the church for forgiveness when caught, shows signs of someone who is spiritually sick. At this point, someone within the leadership should step in to address his positioning and time away from the forefront of the church to get before God in true repentance and position oneself for healing. A repetitive sin is an uncorrected sin. To have true repentance, you must whole-heartedly regret disappointing God because of it.

## Joel 2:12-13 KJV

*"Therefore also now, saith the LORD, turn ye even to me with all your heart, and with fasting, and with weeping, and with mourning: and rend your heart, and not your garments, and turn unto the LORD your God: for he is gracious and merciful, slow to anger, and of great kindness, and repenteth him of the evil."*

Remember one of the key characteristics of a shepherd is to be respectable and respected by outsiders. You should never be in a leadership position and lack respect for God. There is no call of God that allows us to consistently operate in sin, without conviction. If the questionable behavior is consistent without repentance and they choose to stay in that place of disobedience, you need to be attentive and be in prayer. We must show grace and mercy while using wisdom in our walk in Christ. A pastor making a mistake is no reason to leave a church. Doing so hastily would be harsh judgment. However, consider the three C's to determine if you should be asking God if you should stay or leave a ministry.

"You can only do the wrong thing for a short amount of time without it affecting who you are, before it becomes what you are."
-Sharon C. Lenior

1. Consistent Wrongdoing (sin)
2. Compromised Teachings
3. Contradicting Behaviors

These three C's are the evidence that flesh has overrode their godly convictions. Before you make any decision to leave a ministry, you should always, pray first and wait on God to give you directions. Do this without gossiping and speaking to unnecessary people about the details. The type of clarity needed from God in incidents like this, requires us to be still and stay in a position of prayer. Unnecessary conversations about something you are waiting to hear God on can cause a distraction. These distractions often have the same impact as a band randomly playing music in a library. The stillness that is expected in the library is disrupted. Even if someone can work with noise, they usually will no longer do so in this scenario because the environment implied there would be peace and quiet. Once what is expected is disrupted, the usual response is the inability to go back to what they were previously doing.

The stillness needed to hear God's voice is disrupted by the banging of other people's opinions, anger, and natural reactions. You can become so preoccupied with the commotion of the conversations that you don't even realize that the enemy caused you to participate in creating your own distraction. The commotion and outcome of these conversations can often become louder than the voice of God. This can cause you to miss the directive altogether or miss the details in the instructions. The details can include the timing of one's movement.

It is crucial for you to not move at your own volition. Moving out of a place that God has planted you in, without his approval can do more harm than good. If the pastor is out of place and God has already dealt with him behind closed doors but it is unbeknownst to you, not seeing this encounter yourself, may cause you to decide to leave prematurely. Without God's permission and you thinking the pastor didn't fix the problem fast enough can cause you to move out of season.

It is God's timing, not your own. What if God planned to remove him as the pastor if he did not repent, instead of removing you? The last thing you want to do is go somewhere God did not send you. Moving without God's approval can cause you not to complete your assignment, because now, you are out of order and out of alignment. You do not want to make the mistake of jumping in front of God. Remember how long it took you to fix something that you may have struggled with? It is easy to end up in a place of disobedience while trying to do the right thing, by not having the right authorization and timing by God. If your timing is wrong and you never received God's permission, your efforts to do the right thing will be misplaced, incorrect or out of order. If God is the head of your life, you have already agreed to allow him to be the one who leads you. If you believe that your season is up, ask yourself two questions.

1.    Did you complete what God sent you to do?
2.    Did you receive what God sent you to receive?

Do not let the enemy distract you or get you to move out of God's timing.

# Chapter 7

## Choosing Good Ground

It is a significant choice when choosing the right church to call home. One of the worst things that someone can do is jump into a church and become a member because they felt the anointing of God without doing any research on the ministry itself. Yes, you want to be in a house where God moves and breakthroughs and miracles happen, but there's so much more to it. Do your homework, before joining a ministry. Always remember to ask questions and never compromise the *3 Rules of Never*.

There is no way to decide where to be planted if you do not have all the facts. Without having all the facts, your decision is in danger of being based on emotion and feel good moments. You must be sure that the ministry that you are considering believes in the same things you believe in. You must know if they believe in speaking in tongues or if they even allow it in their church if that is part of your spiritual walk. I am still blown away how some churches do not believe in speaking in tongues, though the Bible tells us that this is a gift from the Holy Spirit. Knowing information like this is going to impact decisions for the ministry, especially if you are called to operate in an area that ministry may not believe in. Do your due diligence before submitting somewhere God did not send you.

## Acts 2:4 NLT

*"And everyone present was filled with the Holy Spirit and began speaking in other languages, as the Holy Spirit gave them this ability."*

# The 3 Rules of Never

1. NEVER join a ministry if you do not agree with the vision or direction of the house (church)
2. NEVER join a ministry if you do not believe that the pastor or leaders can lead you in a way that will help you develop and grow in God, ministry or in your gifts. (In short, never join a ministry if you do not trust your pastors.)
3. NEVER join a ministry if God did not finalize/confirm your answer.

Now, I know exactly what you're thinking. You think I am going to give you a deep secret or red flag about what to look for in their ministry, but truth is, this is more about you than them. People make quick decisions about joining churches all the time. Quick decisions do not always mean wrong decisions but there are a few reasons that the *3 Rules of Never* should be taken very seriously. You should not join a church because you think the members are your type of people or just because you think they are friendly to you. When you join a church, you are confirming that you agree with the vision and the shepherd of the house. This is not about your own vision, but your obedience, submission and support building and assisting the working vision that God has already assigned to that church and pastor. To join a ministry that you do not agree with, will put you in a position to go against the Word of God.

The assignment God has already given that shepherd, can leave your hands idle in your calling when in the wrong house. If you fight or rebel against the church vision, even if you do not think you are wrong, you are still operating in disobedience and you are out of order. God says that this will not be favorable to you. Justifying your feelings or behavior will not make you right. God has chosen and given that pastor a mandate for that house (church) in which he was assigned. If you cannot follow the vision or the leadership willingly, that ministry may not be the one for you. Their assignment has already been laid out by God well before your arrival. If you feel the need to buck against the pastor, the vision, the guidelines, or correction, you are opposing what God has set in place and bring judgment on yourself. God's vision is clear. Defiance against the pastor, leaders or church guidelines is out of order if they are correctly aligned with the Word of God.

# Romans 13:2 NLT

*"So anyone who rebels against authority is rebelling against what God has instituted, and they will be punished."*

Regardless of how you may feel about the vision of that house, God has called each church to their own assignment. If you have a ministry of deliverance and know spiritual warfare is part of your ministry, it may not be best for you to be planted in a church whose assignment is significantly based on financial breakthrough. When your insight of the pastor, vision or ministry is full of complaints, you need to check your heart and your purpose of being there. Every church should have some sense of deliverance and warfare know-how but the operation of the church and how it is run will usually reflect their mandate (assignment). Be sure to ask God where you should be planted. Never allow the enemy to make you feel like you're taking one for the team. God created us in spirit and will not assign you somewhere that will not promote spiritual growth, regardless of the position you have been called to serve in.

Being assigned to a position of leadership does not exclude you from learning things that will elevate you to your next level. There should always be room for spiritual growth. Even if your assignment consists of you helping a ministry, it is never one sided. God does not make casualties of war, so no one should experience a spiritual death in a healthy church. This means that despite the assignment, there will always be room for you to learn and grow. Spiritual death can happen gradually by being planted in a church that you cannot recognize as a place of learning or does not build or allow you to operate in your call. Be aware of opinions that encourage you to be comfortable with being spiritually stagnant. Do not allow people to tell you that the reason you are spiritually dying or are stagnant is because it is not your season. There may be times that are not as grand as the next, but a relationship with Christ is exactly that, a relationship. Sometimes, you may feel that everything has been working for your good and other times you may feel like God isn't listening. Though we may not always experience the great side of things, God will not forsake us, so do not discourage during those moments. Wisdom and discernment are necessary when presented with explanations about why you are not growing spiritually. Ensure that the reasoning presented is biblically sound.

There are churches that are called to operate in deliverance. These churches operate in a heavy amount of warfare because they are called to bring people out of some very dark places. These churches usually have some heavy-hitting prayer warriors. Their ministry requires people who know how to reach Heaven and have a prayer life outside of church, constantly building their spiritual strength by praying, fasting and worship. It's like working out in a spiritual gym. Though a deliverance church must be constantly charged up in prayer and ready to battle in the spirit realm, all churches should and need to be prayed up. Prayer is not a luxury, it is a necessity for your spiritual walk, strength, and growth. A church that doesn't have a praying foundation leaves themselves open to make decisions based on what is naturally perceived to be the best decision, instead of the best decisions spiritually decided by God. Prayer is the direct conversation between you and God. It is one of the things needed to be able to recognize his voice.

The assignments that get the worse rap are churches that God has graced for financial breakthroughs and breaking the spirit of poverty. These churches speak on planting seeds and manifestation. God does not want his people to be in debt, nor does he want his people to be in poverty, barely making it. It is a lose-lose situation in the eyes of the world. Anything more than the average car, outfit or even the fact that a pastor has a name brand suit, can be enough reason for people to accuse pastors of living off their offering. Mind you, most of the people with that argument are usually not the ones who are giving a significant offering or one at all. If pastors drove raggedy cars and wore worn out clothes, the argument would be, "If God was so good why aren't you doing better than that?" Truth is, it might take people who are not in seeking a relationship with God a little longer to get out of that cycle with any understanding. It is a waste of time to entertain an argument with people who are determined to find negative things to complain about and not really looking for clarity.

# Chapter 8

## The Inner Workings of the Church

### I Corinthians 12:14 NLT

*"Yes, the body has many different parts, not just one part."*

Imagine an incomplete football team. Normally you would need a stadium, playbook, a team and a coach. Every part of that dynamic has a purpose. Having one without the other doesn't make it impossible to have a game but it does impact the experience and the outcome.

### The Stadium

The church acts as the stadium. This is the place that has been chosen with great thought for location, parking space and amenities. This cannot be decided without considering whether there is enough space for the congregation, enough parking space for visitors and growth. Can it accommodate the congregation for special events, revivals, children's church etc.? This is the place where everyone gathers. Where does the team play if there is no location? This is not about the church building per se' but where people have chosen to gather.

### Acts 17:24 ESV

*"The God who made the world and everything in it, being Lord of heaven and earth, does not live in temples made by man."*

# The Team

The Team is everyone within the ministry that plays a role in the functioning of the church, to include the members and the leadership. This also includes everything from people that are willing to clean the church, mow the grass, clean the bathroom, straighten up the sanctuary, pray over people, set up the media, sing on the choir and everything in-between to keep the church functioning. How do you have a game if there is no one to maintain the things that keep everything running? The people that maintain the church and the ministry are assigned to different areas, but no assignment is too small. Think of all the people who are needed to clean the stadium when the game is over. There are people repainting the lines on the field and those that run the scoreboard. If the scoreboard works but the seats are nasty and unkept, you won't get people to come into the stadium, though they may watch the game from afar. The church has a similar impact. Because the church is God's house, we must treat it as such. Would we allow God to come in if he showed up at the church doors, or would people scramble to make His house presentable? We must take pride in the place that is supposed to be the temple in which we bring our tithes and offering as our sacrifice. When I offer myself to God, sometimes I need to be on my face, crying or laying in his presence. The church floor then becomes the altar in which I give myself to God. We should be mindful of how the altar is presented. We must not take pride in ourselves, but in God's house because this is where we give reverence and honor to God.

## Psalm 84:10 NLT

*"A single day in your courts is better than a thousand anywhere else! I would rather be a gatekeeper in the house of my God than live the good life in the homes of the wicked."*

## The Playbook

The playbook does not really need to be explained in this context. It is the unfailing and unshakable Word of Jesus Christ, the book we all know as the Bible. This is something that should never be compromised. It is okay for people to teach and preach from a subject they found in a book, but it must, without any excuse, be written and founded on the Word of God. Books written with spiritual insight should be written from a place of revelation and scripture. No matter what the subject is, the book should not hold more weight than the Word of God. Anything that cannot be supported by the Word of God is unbiblical or opinion based. This is not acceptable if it cannot stand hand in hand with scripture. A team without a playbook is a team without a plan.

# Romans 15:4 AMP

*"For whatever was written in earlier times was written for our instruction, so that through endurance and the encouragement of the Scriptures we might have hope and overflow with confidence in His promises."*

## The Coach

The coach is the person who gives the directive. They would be the leaders or the pastor in this example. Though everyone understands the assignment at hand, the coach is the one everyone listens to and rallies around for direction and guidance. They tend to be able to explain things in a way that is easily understood whether their newcomers, or someone seasoned. This is a great gift to have, especially if you are a leader. Every good coach will practice patience and consider the level of understanding of those they are teaching. Having patience will allow them to explain the playbook (the Word) to someone who may need more time or deeper explanation of the scriptures (playbook). One person cannot be everything to everybody, everywhere, all the time. If everyone does their part, a team working together can accomplish great things. We are only assistant coaches to the head coach, God. There is nothing that we should do in the Kingdom of God, without guidance from his Word (playbook) or the head coach himself (God). To move without God is to move within self. Understanding how each of these positions work together will allow a church to run smoothly and keeping God as the focal point.

# Chapter 9

## Praise & Worship

Praise and worship are two words that are often used together in church, but do you know the difference? Praise is the act of thanking God, celebrating all that he does and all that he can do. Praise can be shown by praise dancing, raising your hands, shouting, clapping, or singing. Praise can include things that you can do with your body or things that become an extension of you, like drumming or playing a keyboard. God is amazing, so when we praise God, we are saying, "I am joyful in all that you have done, will do and are capable of doing." Praising God allows you to celebrate your awareness of God's existence.

### Psalm 150:6 NLT

*"Let everything that breathes sing praises to the Lord! Praise the Lord!"*

So, what is worship? Worship is a personal and intimate interaction with God. To be able to worship God you must have a relationship with him. You must understand his character and who he is. This means you must make it your business to interact with God through prayer and reading his Word, so that you can connect to God, spirit to spirit. Anyone can praise God, but to worship God is an act of admiration, humbleness, and reverence. To worship God is to have such an admiration for God that you are willing to come to a complete surrender. You cannot know God without having a personal relationship with him. It is impossible to worship God without being saved. It is impossible to worship God without being saved. Worshiping God builds a closeness with him and allows you to get to know him for yourself. Who God is and what God can do is no longer hearsay. Hearsay has now become your own encounters and testimonials of God.

# Chapter 10

## Knowledge is Power

Once saved, you should be making a conscious effort to live in a way that is pleasing to God and according to the Word of God Reading your Bible is also needed to maintain your salvation. At this point, you should be doing your best to follow biblical guidelines. This is how you will know if what you are doing is the right way to do things. The Bible is our spiritual instruction manual. It is the instructions to living a life that God approves of. Every teaching that we embrace should be of sound doctrine. Sound doctrine is teachings that are founded, supported and verified with scripture and conducive with God sacrificing his only son for our sins.

You must read the Bible yourself to recognize false teachings, false prophets, and false context. Reading and studying God's Word prepares you to identify distorted or misinterpreted scripture and doctrine. Our job, as Christians is to lead people to Christ. We must be familiar with the teachings of Christ to avoid saying things that are not biblically sound or spreading hearsay. Our evidence must be solid. When I tell someone that God is a healer, I can walk away from that person confidently knowing that I can show them proof or reference. This doesn't mean that you will be able to tell them the exact scripture and the chapter off the top of your head, but you should be able to share biblical context and references. An example of this is telling someone, "If you read the story of the woman with the issue of blood, you will see how God was able to heal this woman without ever touching her." This opens the door to discuss her faith level or how the length of time that people have been sick means nothing to God. He has no limitations on who, what, when, where and how he chooses to heal. Though you may not be able to give the exact scripture at that moment, you don't want to leave them without a scripture reference for too long. Share with them where they can find that information to solidify that your words are rooted in scripture. When someone asks you to clarify something for them and you do not know the answer to their question, do not wildly guess. Be sure that you have a scriptural foundation. It is always better to be prepared when possible but if not, offering to give them that information as soon as you can is the next best thing. Take a few minutes to look it up or call someone who may be able to help. It is always best to close the gap of misunderstanding by not allowing a lot of time to pass between the initial conversation and providing the supporting scriptures.

## II Timothy 3:16-17 ESV

*All scripture is breathed out by God and profitable for teaching, for reproof, for correction, and for training in righteousness, that the man of God may be complete, equipped for every good work.*

This must be the practice of every Christian to avoid being led down a road that does not line up with the Word of the God. Reading the Word of God should be done continually as you pursue Christ. You cannot effectively lead people to Christ if your familiarity with God's heart is vague. You must be confident in who God is.

I may have mentioned this earlier, but I find it important enough to repeat. No matter how long we have been saved, we should always remain teachable. If we get to a place in our salvation where we are so sure of ourselves that we cannot accept correction or a word from someone spiritually sound, we are spiritually in a dangerous place.

Those who find themselves in this place usually have no idea that they have unknowingly opened a back door to the spirit of pride and false humility. They believe that they are not operating in either one of those spirits, but this is exactly how the enemy is able to work undisturbed in their life. The devil never makes himself obvious. He is calculating and meticulous. He waits until he can see a weakness in your spiritual life and seizes his opportunity. The enemy's tactic can be so subtle that most people do not recognize that they have shifted spiritually. A tell-tell sign is their distorted perception of self-importance.

Those that the enemy has targeted successfully, unknowingly center themselves in things that have nothing to do with them. This is how easily the devil can seize an opportunity to distort or destroy someone's spiritual walk. They may be so sure of themselves that even when something has nothing to do with them personally, they believe that other people's choices, decisions or conversations are influenced by them. The more unaware they are, the more danger they are in spiritually. This is not to say that they cannot recognize all that God has done for them, how anointed they are or what season they are in. The enemy has them so deceived that they don't even recognize that they are operating in false humility. They can have a reverence and love for God in their heart, but that slight shift can start to make them spiritually unhealthy one millimeter at a time. Many who fall into this spiritual trap will start to show signs in their walk with God. These symptoms can be anything from a decrease in their prayer life to an arrogance that they don't realize others can see. The list could go on. The enemy uses these opportunities to shift their focus from God to themselves so seamlessly, that they don't even notice how often they feel the need to make themselves relevant in other people's dealings.

It does not matter how many times someone teaches Samson and Delilah or Daniel in the Lion's Den; you will notice that each time a different person preaches it, there is a new revelation or insight. No matter what new revelation is revealed, be careful of what revelations you are absorbing and supporting. Titles and pulpits do not certify the message, the Word of God does.

The enemy will sneak one in on you if he can. Attention to detail is just as vital in understanding the Word of God as it is in following it. We are to spread the news of his goodness and should follow no one blindly but God. This means until we can verify what people are saying, we are to accept it with prejudice. There have been many pastors that have fallen from their positions due to sin or have compromised their assignment at the expense of gaining members. Many have allowed the church and their teachings to be influenced by the ways of the world instead of the world being influenced by the Word of God. Many have compromised their salvation for inclusion and windows of opportunity by allowing certain sins to be accepted in their church. People have adopted and accepted these ungodly behaviors because it allows them to stay in their sin and made to feel like God is okay with it. This is why we should not just sit through the preaching without listening intently to ensure that it lines up with the Word of God. What is acceptable in someone's church does not mean it is acceptable in God's eyes. You must be willing to do the research when you have questions or concerns. Find out what scripture they are coming from and then read it for yourself to ensure that the interpretation has not been misinterpreted. This usually means that you must read the before and after verses to be sure that you have the correct understanding. There are scriptures, when read alone, that can be misunderstood. My own personal practice when studying is to read 3 to 5 scriptures before and after the verse I am studying. Once you read the prior and following verses in its entirety, you may realize those verses were for a particular group of people or time. It may not have pertained to you at all.

If you believe that something has been misinterpreted during a sermon, you should pursue clarity from a leader at a time that will not cause confusion. Asking for a leader to explain something a little bit more in depth, works best during a Bible study rather than a typical service. A Bible study is usually a little less formal and is a great time to ask for clarity or reference if the pastor allows it. Requesting clarity for understanding is okay even if you have a different interpretation or disagree. Sometimes one of you can be wrong or both of you could be right based on one's understanding. Having a desire to understand God's heart and the Word of God will often lead people to ask questions instead of leaning into their own understanding. Be patient with them, this can be a great opportunity for learning. You do not want to cause anyone else any confusion in a group setting if the question can not be clarified in a reasonable amount of time. The Pastor may want to continue the conversation one on one to ensure you get it. If the person teaching encourages you to continue the conversation, do not be ashamed or disheartened if you still do not understand. Sometimes you are the vessel in which God has chosen to speak up for someone you probably didn't even know had the same question but were too scared to ask. God is very intentional that way.

How you handle your concern or questions is the difference between asking for clarity and challenging a leader. A humble approach resembles the willingness to listen to learn, instead of hearing to debate. Do not go into a situation that needs clarity with the intent of schooling your teacher or leader. Even if they're completely wrong in their interpretation, so is your heart posture. Even if their interpretation is not exact, your approach may be the only thing wrong in that scenario. Ask questions to learn something, not to prove something. Be mindful that everyone will not be on the same level of understanding so be patient and gentle with your words.

## I Peter 3:15 NASB

*"But sanctify Christ as Lord in your hearts, always being ready to make a defense to everyone who asks you to give an account for the hope that is in you, yet with gentleness and respect."*

Approach every question asked as an opportunity to help educate someone on the details of Christ. Our answers can be correct, but if you are a logical thinker and the person asking is a creative thinker, they may not understand your explanation no matter how many times you explain it. Someone can walk up to them and give them a creative example and in two minutes they understand what you been explaining to them for over an hour. It may not have had anything to do with your ability to explain, but their compatible style of learning. Ministering to people of different ages, recognizing cultural differences and spiritual upbringings are all things that can impact the ability to explain and understand biblical foundation. These things can act like a language barrier and cause frustration or a feeling of defeat. Being able to give someone the clarity they need and making sure they are confident with their understanding of the Word can be all that stands between their "no" or "yes" to God. Always remember that.

Approach teaching like you are learning a new way to communicate with someone who speaks a different language. This will mentally demand that you challenge yourself to different ways of teaching for different types of students. If you are the teacher of a Bible study and you believe that no one can tell you about the subject you are teaching, you have already counted God out. God can use anyone to get his point across. Sometimes God will use the person who doesn't understand as much as you, to humble you. You may be expecting to be the only one teaching a lesson but sometimes the thing you need to learn has nothing to do with your Bible study subject. The students may be learning about order, while God may be teaching you patience.

Your learning experience may be in the process. That one question that may be so simple to you, may be the question that God uses to reveal to you that people may need you to slow down, or go spend a little more time on the basics. Good teaching in the Kingdom is not based on how educated you sound to other people. It's not about impressing the visiting pastor or guest. Good teaching is not leaving anybody spiritually left behind. You should teach with the intention of not allowing anyone to walk out the door feeling empty-handed. There are some people who will pick this book up and think, I am well beyond what this book is teaching and that may be true. However, I don't believe anyone who is reading this book is reading it by happenstance. Sometimes we can preach and teach over people's heads without even realizing it. Not everyone will raise their hand when they have a question or tell you that you lost them when you said, "This is a Five-Fold Ministry." Some of us have been in ministry for so long that the church lingo and terms are etched in our memory. The question is, can we really explain those terms to someone else or have we just gotten so used to hearing them that we haven't given the meaning much thought?

I grew up in a Christian home and recall being part of a Five- Fold Ministry as a child. Every church I went to as an adult, I made sure that it was also a Five-Fold Ministry. It wasn't until I was well into my late 30's that I even understood exactly what that meant. If the church claimed they were a Five-Fold ministry, that was enough for me. I was okay not knowing what that really meant. That's just how much I trusted my upbringing as a child. I wouldn't suggest taking the "following blindly" approach though. It's by the grace of God, my mother's first pastor, Elder Louis Bowers, and my grandfather, Reverend Joseph Theophilus Freeman, made sure my parents were spiritually grounded in their teens. This allowed me to grow up in a household that made sure that what we learned was rooted in the Word of God. My parents did things the right way, but not all kids can say that. As an adult, I had to learn through church hurt and spiritual maturity that it is wise not to follow anyone blindly but God. I know better now and require all others show me the proof. Not fully understanding certain aspects of ministry has become the hush-hush position of many Christians and we have to stop allowing this to be the norm. We are willing to sit amongst people that share the same beliefs as we do, without a real understanding of all that we believe in.

You cannot get to know God if you are building your relationship with him based only on rumors. When you read God's Word for yourself, understand it, and start applying it to your life, you will also experience the benefits and encounters that are expressed in his Word. That within itself is the receipt and proof that God is real. You must have a deeper understanding of God to experience everything that comes with a life of salvation. There is no such thing as living a partial life of salvation and still receiving the full benefits of being saved. Anything done partially can never be approached as if it has been done in whole. The Word of God says, we cannot serve light and dark at the same time. You want to be in an environment that is conducive with the miracles and wonders of God? Get to know God. There are people who have never accepted Christ or have turned away from God, who can quote or know scripture. Knowing scriptures doesn't mean they know God, it means they know better.

## I John 2:3-4 NLT

*And we can be sure that we know him if we obey his commandments. If someone claims, "I know God," but doesn't obey God's commandments, that person is a liar and is not living in truth.*

## James 1:22 KJV

*"But be ye doers of the word, and not hearers only deceiving your own selves."*

Christians should be actively listening and doing according to his Word. Things that are learned but not applied will not earn you a credit with God. To think the only insight we need is our own puts a target on our back that the enemy can see a mile away. We need other brothers and sisters to help keep us grounded, humbled and honest with ourselves. This will keep us at an angle that allows us to see any plank that may be in our own eyes before pointing out the splinter in someone else's.

# Chapter 11

## To Church or Not to Church?

## Hebrew 10:25 ESV

*"Not neglecting to meet together, as is the habit of some, but encourages ones another, and all the more as you see the Day drawing near."*

We are required to practice what we preach and not just play the part. This leads people to ask if you have to go to church to be saved? The simple answer is no, but not without explanation. It is not a requirement to go to church to be saved but it is a requirement to stay on the right track. This helps ensure that you do not compromise your salvation. Churches are not perfect. They operate spiritually in the same way a hospital operates for the sick. People who go to the hospital do not go because they are healthy, they go to get healthy or to stay healthy. Those that are already healthy, go to maintain a healthy life. This is the same concept for churches. You will sometimes hear people combat going to church because they can read the Word for themselves. They believe that they can grow in God without any outside assistance. Though our relationship with God is a personal one, no one can live that life for us. You also cannot teach yourself what you do not know. No matter how comfortable we are with being self-taught, there are some subjects that are too crucial to leave to our own understanding. The most important subject is our salvation and the Bible. Salvation is not something you want to risk to your own understanding. You know why you wouldn't teach yourself how to be an electrician? Because getting it wrong can be the difference between life and death. Salvation has the same impact spiritually if you don't get it right. Is that something you would want to risk?

There are things in the Word of God that a new Christian and even some seasoned Christians (people who have longevity in Christ) may not spiritually be in a place to understand. How long you have been saved does not determine where you are spiritually. There are those that have been saved for years and have never achieved a higher level in God. I used to be one of those people. I had a checklist of everything I was and was not supposed to do as a Christian. I checked off the boxes mentally. I knew I should not get drunk; curse and I should attend church on Sunday's. For years I followed the formula, never really understanding how to pursue God after I got saved. I had witnessed people speaking in tongues and excelling in the Kingdom months after they were saved, while others had been saved for years and had never spoken in tongues or showed any growth in God. I recognized my own people, the ones who were living by the imaginary Christian checklist.

I finally realized that it is not how long you have been saved that excels your spiritual relationship with God, it is the consistency and the pursuit of God. There are things you may read in the Word that seem like common sense, but as you further your relationship with Christ, you will be in a place for a spiritual and deeper understanding. Think about it, even if you read about being saved, you probably still felt the need for someone to explain it a little better. Even if this is the first time you read about being saved, giving examples and explaining in detail helps those reading this book build confidence in their understanding. No one is incapable of reading and understanding on their own, but everyone is capable of getting it wrong. Sometimes we need to gather with the saints because we need a little extra covering in prayer, an insightful testimony for encouragement or a prophetic word of details for our next move in our season. If God is telling us not to forsake it, the devil will encourage us to do the opposite.

# Chapter 12

## What is a Five-Fold Ministry?

Y ou may have been sitting in church or out and about and have heard someone say that the church they attend is a Five-Fold Ministry and wondered what they meant. This term is one that is used throughout the Christian community so often that when it is used, no one thinks that it needs to be explained. Sometimes, we think because we are in the House of God, that all terminology regarding church needs no break down. We must remember that not everyone in the congregation is saved, familiar or fluent with the words that come so naturally to some. I think it is wise to make sure that we know spiritually where the congregation is, especially if it is our own. That's a little harder to do when you are at someone else's church, but if you are speaking, it is best to assume that no one there has an understanding. That will ensure you to preach at a level that even the new Christians can walk away with complete understanding.

So, what is a Five-Fold Ministry? This is a ministry that is built on the structure that God has intended for his house. There are five specific pillars that God says he has gifted to equip and build the church. These five pillars are Apostles, Prophets, Evangelist, Pastors and Teachers. Each one of those roles plays a vital part in the spiritual structure of the church.

# Ephesians 4:11-13 NLT

*"...Now these are the gifts Christ gave to the church: the apostles, the prophets, the evangelist, and the pastors and teachers. Their responsibility is to equip God's people to do his work and build up the church, the body of Christ. This will continue until we all come to such unity in our faith and knowledge of God's Son that we will be mature in the Lord, measuring up to the full and complete standard of Christ."*

1.  **Apostles** often act as overseers and lead the way into new endeavors. Pioneers.

2.  **Prophets** are often called to deliver a revelation, give a warning or provide guidance from God. They often deliver messages and speak about what God is saying and his will for the people. Though everyone is held to account when they do not deliver a message from God, Prophets are held to a higher standard because this is the purpose of their position. Ezekiel 3:17-19, states that God has assigned watchmen to deliver his warning, and that God will hold you accountable for their blood if you do not deliver them. Not completing your assignment is not something you want to have to explain to God.

3.  **Evangelist** often focuses on leading new believers to the church. They often spread the gospel and show strength when it comes to people, especially in areas like outreach in the community. Definitely, a people-person.

4.  **Pastors** are the people that God has chosen to govern his house (church). He cares for the congregation, offering support, spiritual covering and guidance. This is a hard responsibility because it can be difficult to find a balance between the church and home when dealing with different congregation sizes, the need of the people and types of people. Requires a healthy relationship with God, self-awareness, self-evaluations and the ability to correct in love.

5.  **Teachers** often have a natural rhythm for breaking down instructions or explaining things. They thrive in a church that allows room for them to instruct and educate others on sound doctrine and scriptural truth.

# Ezekiel 3:17-19 ESV

*"Son of man, I have made you a watchman for the house of Israel; Whenever you hear a word from my mouth, you shall give them warning from me. If I say to the wicked, 'you shall surely die,' and you give him no warning, nor speak to warn the wicked from his wicked way, in order to save his life, that wicked person shall die for his iniquity, but his blood I will require at your hand. But if you warn the wicked, and he does not turn from his wickedness, or from his wicked way, he shall die for his iniquity, but you will have delivered your soul."*

# Chapter 13

## The Call vs. The Ministry

What is the difference between your ministry and your call? Though they are continuously mixed up, there are so many people that don't have a clear understanding of the difference. I am going to give you a simple response to what sounds like a complicated question.

Your calling is something that God has put you on this Earth to do. I know you're thinking this is the same as ministry but this where it differs. God created each one of us with a specific purpose. Our call is not what we enjoy doing but what God has created us to do. So that leaves the question, what is ministry? Ministry is our how. The thing that God has created us for still has to be fulfilled. Where our call is our purpose on this Earth, our ministry is the means in which we do it. Ministry is the execution or process in which we plan to fulfill our call. Here is my personal experience with how I found out what my call is and what my ministry is.

My gifts were the reason I was so confused about what I was called to do. I constantly would say to God, "I am capable of doing so many things, but what is my purpose?" It took someone that I was coming out of a relationship with, to say to me, "I do not want to be with someone who is always helping people," to realize what I was created for. I was shocked, devastated and hurt. I was in tears talking to my mother when I told her what had been said. Though this was not the reason for the end of our relationship, it was a blow to my heart to know that the one thing that shaped me as a person, was the same characteristic that my partner seen as a negative. I was always so caring and giving. I cried behind closed doors and expressed to my mom what was in my heart. I told her, "Mom, I do not understand. That's what I do, I help people. To say that he does not want to be with someone who is always helping people is no different than him saying he has never loved me because that's who I have always been. That's who I am." My mom comforted me, but for weeks after that those words kept replaying in my head. One day the revelation hit me out of nowhere. I was called to help people. That was the one thing that had been consistent in my life and I always felt compelled to do so. It was like I was hit in the face with a steel bat.

All the different ways that I was helping people was the ministry used to operate in my call. God may have given you the call to help women because of your experience with domestic violence, firsthand or as a bystander. The program that you created to help them find housing or a therapy class to build their self-esteem would be the ministry that you have chosen to help them. Someone else may have recognized that there are plenty of programs that help single mothers but none for single fathers. Creating a program that helps single fathers would be the ministry, the heart to help single parents would be the call. Ministry is not limited to just things that pertain to your call. I did not know what my call was, because I did not have a complete understanding of what it truly meant. While what my ex said hurt me to my core; the opportunity that the enemy took to destroy my confidence and question myself, God used for his glory. It was in that harsh moment that I understood what God created me to do. That was my call, but what was my ministry?

My call required me to submit to God and humble my flesh and my own desires to recognize the opportunities God would allow me to have. I started serving in a children's church and ran into kids younger than twelve who were suicidal and broken. No one even knew these things were going on within the four walls of the House of God. Once my supervisor shared a letter that she had found from one of the children, the Holy Spirit told us there were more. I gave some of the older children each a piece of paper and asked a few questions, but 4 questions were more crucial than the others?

1. Do you know someone who has committed suicide?
2. Have you ever thought about committing suicide and why?
3. Do you know someone who wants to commit suicide?
4. What is the name of those people?

I was not surprised to see some of the answers, but I was surprised to see that a few of their answers consisted of other children in our church. Some of those children named weren't even in my class and some were even younger than the age group I was teaching. It was heartbreaking that as adults, some of these kids, we would automatically deem too young to even need to have an in-depth conversation on that subject. The worst part was the parents had no clue. The best part was I was in the right position, because of my obedience to get involved. I submitted to my call and accepted my rightful place in ministry. I was there to help them. I helped them spiritually by interceding on their behalf, covering them, teaching them how to pray, and empowering them to deal with their everyday hurdles effectively. That was spiritually my responsibility but naturally I felt the push to do more. I asked God for guidance and created a bullying program to address the cause of these issues. My supervisor and I notified the pastor and he took it out of our hands.

I never felt burdened to encourage them, love them and cover them. It was something that God had placed inside of me before birth, to help the forgotten. Had I not been obedient, I would not have been positioned for them to tell me things that they hadn't told anybody else besides their friends. My ability to explain things on a more simplified level allowed me to reach them in ways that they expressed others could not. It brought me joy in writing programs for children and women who had lost their way or given up on themselves and life. Teaching them to find their voice, creating a program that reached them and showed them how to fight spiritually; while providing natural steps that would help change their mindsets. This was ministry. I was birthed for this. Teaching was my ministry. Writing this book is my ministry. Writing spoken word and worship music is my ministry. Interceding in prayer is my ministry. My ministry is everything that I use as a transportation service to support my call.

Being in a ministry and operating in your ministry are two different things. Keep in mind, it is God who has created us for purpose so be sure you are operating how and where God called you to be. There is more than one ministry that can assist you in your calling, so do not get too worked up if you are not involved in a specific ministry. This can be tough because people tend to stop serving in other areas of ministry if it is not their preference. You never know if the ministry you are operating in will be a teaching ground to prepare you for your next level. If you are desiring to operate in a certain ministry and your pastor is not in agreement with the timing or the placement, do not be easily angered. God has appointed that shepherd over your spiritual journey and your assignment. God will give that leader the directives, timing and any other details needed for this type of movement. This is not the same thing as when you are searching for a church. You should have vetted by now if that was the church and the Pastor that God has assigned for your covering.

A pastor not letting you preach because you have not shown yourself faithful in other areas is not him trying to keep you from operating in your call. There may still be processes and procedures that need to be followed. That shepherd is accountable for approving your positioning within the House of God and giving you wise counsel, all while still protecting the rest of the sheep. His job requires him to guard the access to the flock and what they are exposed to. Premature movements or timing can impact the church or hinder you or others spiritually. This is something that pastors must answer to God for, so allow your pastor to do his job. God says that he has appointed the authorities that exist, so be careful that you do not allow the enemy to shift your heart posture into rebellion because of your impatience and decision making based on anxiousness.

# Romans 13:1 NASB

*"Every person is to be subject to the governing authorities. For there is no authority except from God, and those which exist are established by God."*

# Philippians 4:6-7 NLT

*Don't worry about anything; instead, pray about everything. Tell God what you need and thank him for all he has done. Then you will experience God's peace, which exceeds anything we can understand. His peace will guard your hearts and minds as you live in Christ Jesus.*

When God gives us revelation it is not always for the right now. Continue to put your hands to the plow for the Kingdom and things will fall into place. If you are under the right pastor, your pastor's prayers will reach heaven, and he will clearly hear the voice of God for directions. Be patient. You do not want to move out of order for the sake of ministry. Moving out of timing and out of disobedience will never work in your favor despite your reasoning, because God is not the author of confusion. Once you shift into a place of rebellion, you hinder yourself and delay your own ministry.

For you to complete the assignment God is requiring of you, you must walk and operate in purpose on purpose. This means to be intentional with how we operate in our purpose (calling). You must choose to serve God wholeheartedly and consistently work toward your purpose. Let's review.

1. What is the definition of your calling based on what you just read?
2. What is the definition of ministry based on what you read?
3. Is ministry or your call considered transportation?
4. What new revelation have you had so far?
5. What do you believe you were called to do?
6. Write down ideas for your ministry?

# Chapter 14

## The Face of a Christian & the Heart of God

Sometimes, the opinions and attitudes of Christians can be louder than the voice of God. This is something that all pastors and leaders should be on alert for. People's opinions cannot override showing the love and compassion of Jesus Christ. The wrong attitude and the wrong people in position can make or decrease the church's growth as a whole or a particular ministry within the church.

Everyone can be polite and kind but not everyone can be a door greeter. You should be careful when allowing people who openly admit that they do not like to deal with people to be in a ministry that requires it. This is not because this is a sin but because whether people are spiritually in the right place or not, visitors may judge the church based on the first thing they see. Someone who doesn't like to deal with people will not have the same demeanor as someone who loves to socialize and is generally a joyful person. Decisions like this must be looked at spiritually because there are people who have been in bondage for so long that they no longer resonate with joy and just need some help getting back to that place. Discernment and timing will always play a part in all decisions in a healthy church. Remember, the people in a ministry are not only a representative of God but also a representative of the church. If they have a nasty attitude, their nasty attitude will meet the guest at the door before the Christ in them does. They have already displayed a negative depiction of who God is supposed to be to those who don't know any better. We are the face of Christ, just like someone who becomes the face of a company. If people don't like the messenger, they already prejudge the message. Do not allow yourself to be the hurdle someone must get pass to get what they came to receive. Sometimes we are the first encounter of Christ that someone has and can very much so be their last. Now ask yourself, how well do you think you represent Christ?

Christianity has taken a great hit in what that word consists of. The word Christianity has been watered down to convince people that all you have to do is believe the stories of the bible to be a Christian. The definition of Christianity is a follower of Christ. You can have Christian beliefs, but living out those beliefs in your own life is what defines you as a Christian. You would never call someone an electrician just because they believe in electricity. It is really that simple. Being a Christian is not just something God gives you credit for because you claim it. Your actions must align with your words. As you take on this lifestyle of Christianity you will realize that it carries a lot of responsibility. God relies on us to represent him in the best way possible and not be ashamed of the man who died on the cross for our sins.

## Matthew 10:33 KJV

*"But whosoever shall deny me before men, him will I also deny before my Father which is in heaven."*

We would never want God to be ashamed of us, so we must not be ashamed of him. We should eagerly be willing to speak of how great God is because of our love and respect for him. Our relationship with him should be something that we proudly profess. The scripture says, if we deny Christ, God will deny us. Wouldn't it be a shame to miss out on going to Heaven because we denied him? Is that a price you're willing to pay? Jesus paid it all for us, and his father, our God, thought we were worth saving, despite what sins had been committed. God is more than a conversation piece and something to brag about and we must treat him as such.

Declare and say out loud:

I am a Child of God.
Uncompromised, unwavering,
prayerful and faithfully rooted in His Word.

I stand before him, humbled that he sees me fit
to serve and represent him.
I lay before him because I am not worthy
to deserve all that he has done,
but his grace and mercy
makes room for me at the cross.

I kneel before him because I am honored
That he knows my name and catches
every tear that I have ever shed.

I am not just a believer but also a doer.
I will continue to spread the good news,
stories of his mercy and grace, signs and wonders,
miracles of healing and testimonies of overcoming
dark and distant places.

I am grateful that he sees me fit
and that he has never forsaken me.
And thankful that as long as he is my
Lord and Savior, Jesus Christ,
the head of my life,
he will continue to mold me and make me.

I am his and he is mine and no one else's.
I am the Child of the Most High God.
Never left alone without his covering,
I am always sheltered.
Uncompromised, unwavering,
prayerful and faithfully rooted in his Word.

These are the benefits of being a true Christian that loves and follows God whole heartedly. There must be a standard for us as representatives of Christ. Do not be the one who taints God's name with your poor behavior or nasty acting character. Self-discipline is a needed to not be baited by the enemy's attacks to discourage you and have you act out of character. Without self-discipline and God, you will always fall for the trap of the enemy because he will continue to bait you with things that cause you to act ungodly. Finding ways to anger you is the oldest trick in the book. The enemy may bait you by messing with your finances to trigger depression, have your kids act up so your language is negative or anything that will allow you to be more receptive to the devil's tactics. Do not fall for it. You must build up your spirit to recognize and shut down the plot from the enemy, even at your weakest moments. Strengthen your spirit with prayer, fasting, reading the Word, worship and praise and speaking in tongues.

Hard times do not function as permission slips or get-out-of-Christ free cards. There is no get-out-of-Christ free card and people who intentionally operate with this mentality think that they can represent God when it's convenient. We are talking about your salvation here. At what cost are you willing to deny God for a moment of self-gratification? Is an eternity of misery worth a moment of glorified sin?

We must be conscious of the enemies' tactics to derail the arrival of our rightful destination. When the enemy can cause you to act out of character, his goal is to set you back twice as far as you have advanced forward. Not everyone can recover to the last place they were standing before they got off their path. Here's an active visual to show you exactly what I mean. Find a volunteer. Do not explain the exercise to them but ask them to do whatever comes natural to them while assisting you. It's important that their response is a natural one to successfully witness the devil's plan.

With a partner, have them stand face to face with you as if you're having a conversation. Tell them they don't have to do anything special, just do what naturally comes to them. Without any warning, but not too much force, push their shoulder or chest. What was their reaction? Did you notice that they stepped back? This is what happens to you spiritually when the enemy's tactics are effective. Once he can get you to react, he's caused you to take a step or two back, but maturity in Christ will push back against your flesh. Your flesh is going to tell you to live in shame, guilt and regret. The only feeling that is acceptable is the conviction of the Holy Spirit, which should follow up with you asking for repentance. Once you do this, the enemy will try to replay that moment to keep you in a place that makes you feel unworthy. Don't allow the enemy to hold you hostage with this tactic. Let it go the moment that you repent. To allow that feeling of guilt or unworthiness to keep you from going forward, the enemy not only caught you in the first trap, but now has you hostage in the second trap. Who cares if the devil remembers what God has already forgotten? When did the devil ever become that relevant.

Once the enemy knocks you back, discouragement will be used to keep you from pushing forward. This is when one of the enemy's most reliable comment comes up. "If it's not one thing, it's another." That term alone tells the enemy that you are feeling the pressure, and he is wearing you down. That comment tells him not to let up because you are at your breaking point, weakened and not at your best. In other words, your position of prayer has been compromised. In a war situation, you have allowed the enemy to take over your position, which is equivalent to there being a security breach in your sector (area). This can cause a weakened area of covering within your home and even in the church. The enemy does not attack to impact just one area of your life. If you are only feeling it in one place, then the enemy is still trying to get his footing. If you feel it in multiple areas of your life, this is a huge sign that he can't find a specific way to get you off track, so he is in panic mode, attacking everything at once. Another reason is because your godly obedience is going to be explosive to the enemies plan so you must be stopped. At this point, his tactic is to attack everything until you get so frustrated that you start to give him a progress report. Some people believe that the devil can hear the thoughts in your head, but the truth is he can't. The devil has no idea that all his attempts to break your spirit are working until you open your mouth to complain. What you say out loud is your declaration. This is why you must guard your words and understand why God says you have the power to declare things over your life. The devil does not understand the impact of his attempts until you confirm with your words or your behavior. We don't report to the enemy, so stopping updating him on which one of his tactics are most effective in your life.

## Proverbs 18:21 ESV

*"Death and life are in the power of the tongue, and those who love it will eat its fruits."*

# Chapter 15

## Symptoms of Spiritual Sickness

Symptoms of spiritual sickness can come in many ways. The enemy's job is to steal, kill and destroy. The greater the purpose the closer you are to the top of the enemy's hit list. God's purpose for you motivates the devil to derail your path. The devil does not waste his time on nobody's. If the enemy can derail you, he can sever the many ties and connections that God has specifically created you to impact. The enemy will pull all the stops to get you to compromise your salvation. You must be aware when your salvation is under attack. Every day we naturally battle the enemy's attempt to tempt us with things of this world. That's something we deal with on a regular basis, but what shifts it from temptation to spiritual sickness?

An issue that can compromise your salvation or your character can cause you to become sick in the spirit. Example, the enemy can put thoughts of perversion in your mind. How? Our flesh is of this world; this world is controlled by the devil. The devil will send his demons to entice our flesh, so the spirit of perversion bombards your mind with sexually explicit thoughts. The enemy has no idea if his tactics worked until you act on it or speak it out of your mouth. The moment you give the enemy access is when you take the bait or do not correct the thought. As you leave the thought unchecked, it gains more and more room in our minds and allows vivid thoughts in detail. If perversion is the spiritual sickness, it can cause you to reminisce about prior sexual experiences that are ungodly. This can be thoughts outside of your spouse or past sexual encounters that were not sanctioned under the covenant of marriage. Unchecked attacks like this from the enemy will cause your spiritual walk to be compromised. The devil's proof that his attacks have been successful is when you start to experience behaviors like perverse speech, interest in pornography, masturbation, and sexual thoughts that you can no longer control. There will always be symptoms in someone's walk when they have been spiritually compromised. The symptoms will be evident way before your spirit becomes completely sick. This subject goes much deeper than this, but I'll save that for another time. Not being able to recognize the red flags in your own walk can disrupt your ministry, and the ministries that you are tied to. Your walk is not just about you, but those who are spiritually tied to you through ministry and encounters. You must continually check your spirit. It's part of your spiritual maintenance. Any one person who cannot see their own flaws or think they are so far along in Christ that there is no room for them to make a mistake is in dangerous territory.

Self-discipline, self-awareness and worship are 3 effective tools that can be paired with prayer to counter-act the enemy's game plan. You must be aware of the sharpest tools in your spiritual toolbox. Self-discipline allows you to kill the enemies plan the moment him and his demonic minions attempt to disrupt your spirit, but timing is everything. Worship is a powerful tool because worship confuses the enemy. The devil has no understanding of why you would be praising God at a time that he feels like he has given you enough to complain or curse God about. Not only does worship confuse the enemy, but it also strengthens your spirit as you trail through what may be a difficult storm. Yes, there are other tools that are effective but everything in God is effective. So, this is not a dismissal of the obvious, just some keys that I can personally say have been effective in a big way. The right worship music, the right heart and honesty with God will break somethings off of you. It can also shift an atmosphere, especially when you are experiencing a sense of heaviness and don't know what to pray. One of my favorite things about studying the Word is when God gives me a simplistic gem to explain a revelation. One of my favorites is the enemy attacks our flesh to break our spirit. This is such a simplistic way of understanding the devils plot while spotlighting how he plans to do it.

This is why the devil will attack your health, finances and even your children. Sometimes the enemy throwing a small hurdle in front of someone can cause them to abandon everything they stand on. Have you ever encountered someone who claims to be a Christian but every time they get upset, they resemble everything that doesn't resemble Christ? This is a prime example of someone who needs to strengthen their spirit. A small hurdle shouldn't trigger you to sin if your spirit is stronger than your flesh. No Christian is perfect, however if you find yourself falling victim to the bait, there is something lacking in your spiritual walk. It is most likely not enough time in prayer or studying the Word of God. When you study your Word and pray, you strengthen your spirit. Because our flesh is of this world and I John 5:19, says the world around us is under the control of the evil one. If we are not praying and studying the Word consistently, our spirit is weakened. Not feeding your spirit will always strengthen your flesh. This is when the enemy seizes the opportunity to provoke you, allowing the devil an opportunity to attack. Positioning and length of salvation does not exclude you from the enemies plan to reacquaint you with your old sinful nature.

I had an encounter where the enemy tempted me with a trigger that had me fighting my flesh like Mike Tyson fighting his opponent. God had delivered me over 10 years ago from grudges and anger that I could keep for more than a decade. My godly conviction didn't allow my flesh to completely dominate the situation, but my lack of prayer allowed room for my flesh to make a cameo appearance. That would have never happened if I had stayed in my Word and prayed instead of sulking during a very difficult time. My godly convictions demanded me to repent for my actions within seconds. That part was a quick resolve, but the hard part was not allowing the devil to guilt me with feelings of being unworthy. I reminded myself, "you weren't perfect when God called you the first time." The devil remembers what God has forgotten. Ignore him.

## Chapter 16

## Right Place, Wrong Time

The impact that an unbeliever and a compromised Christian can have when wrongly positioned in the church can be detrimental to the ministry. There are many leaders that let this one slip through the cracks until they must clean up something that could have been avoided with early on correction. By not addressing an issue in a timely manner, it can unknowingly give the devil a window of opportunity. Indirectly, it is equivalent to holding back the curtains for him as he climbs through the window because he dares not enter through the front door. The biggest area of ministry that this happens in more frequently than others is the music ministry. It's unfortunate that the music ministry is one of the easiest targets for the devil to infiltrate but it's not without reason. In the scripture Ezekiel 28:13, satan was created with instruments inside of him. No other angel was described this way. This demonstrates that the devil had some internal tie to music. If you pay attention to the sound and the words in today's music and the spiritual position of the artist, you will notice that the enemy isn't even trying to hide anymore. He is bold with intentions and secular artist have outwardly said that they worship satan and declare their positions in the demonic realm as witches and warlocks.

I recall watching a video of a secular artist who started his concert by telling his fans, "We all going to hell today." As some of the crowd started to disagree with his comment, he continued to tell them it was too late and that they had already been listening to his music. On other videos of this same concert, people were falling out as demons took over their body. People don't realize that music can usher in demonic spirits just like worship music ushers in the Holy Spirit. People get so caught up with the beat or rhythm of a song, that they ignore the lyrics. Think about it, when you play sad break-up songs, it creates an atmosphere of depression and sadness. When you want to heal and move on, you start playing songs that empower and encourage you to be your best in singleness. We naturally use music to create an atmosphere for our emotions and our spirit. This is why leaders must be careful who they let stand on their pulpits speaking and singing over their congregation. Just as that secular artist told his fans, it's too late to get away, he openly admits that he serves the devil, and he planned on taking his fans to hell with him. Even if he was singing that he just wants to be in love, because of his demonic positioning as a satanist, the lyrics to his song could very much so include curses within the words or in the sound of the music due to the demons that influenced it's creation. Curses can also be hidden in background music, lower frequencies or whispers to keep you from noticing. The first thing I saw regarding that secular artist came from a girl that was recording a video as she was walking out of the concert. She asked everyone who was watching, "Do y'all hear the sound that is coming out of the speakers?" She proceeded to say she didn't want anyone to even hear it because it sounded like demons. She said she couldn't stay and had to get out of there. I believe she had enough spiritual insight along the way that she recognized that there was a demonic encounter happening and she needed to leave immediately. I believe someone was covering this young lady in prayer. I am also praying for her salvation in God. Sometimes it's not obvious to everyone or from the beginning that the devil is at work. When that artist was singing, he was releasing curses and demons over people. He didn't tell the fans that it was too late because they were already in the building. He told them they were too late because they had already been listening to his music well before that concert. People were exposed to demonic influences and some of them had no idea until those demons no longer felt the need to hide. The same situation can happen if the pastor is not mindful of the condition of his members.

Within the last four days, I went to a fundraiser for my niece's school choir. It was a dinner and a show that was being held at one of our local churches. Though it was not my niece's choir that was singing, she was there as a server to do her part in the fundraiser. As the featured choir sang and people came up one by one to do their solo, what started off great quickly shifted. They sang old school songs like Frank Sinatra, other secular artists and songs that came from Tim Burton cartoons that are known for their gothic themes. For this to be their first show, their voices were amazing but that was quickly overshadowed with the choice of song. During one performance, a young man stood at the front of the church fellowship hall with a warlock cloak on. As he began to sing, two people with the same cloak came down the aisle from the back of the room with their heads down, holding microphones in front of them with both hands and singing what sounded like a demonic chant. I immediately looked at my mom and sister and said, "They are releasing a curse and opening demonic portals." We immediately began to pray. I could see the pastor and his wife obviously bothered the moment they heard the word "witch" come out of their mouths, exchanging glances of concern, but they never moved. You could tell by their faces that they were not approving of the song, and it seemed to catch them by surprise. I am unsure if they didn't stop it because it was a school function or they just didn't want to make a scene. As the song spoke of holding death's hand, calling on spirit guides and opening dark hidden doors, I was so concerned with the souls that were unaware of what was happening. I don't think those attending knew the spiritual magnitude of what was going on, but their faces also showed concern and shock. Some of them moved uncomfortably in their chairs, looking around the room as if they were looking for someone to verify what they were feeling. They knew that this performance should not be happening, especially in a church.

After praying for every attempt to open a portal wouldn't succeed and declared covering over the church and those in attendance, my heart was broken that this openly demonic attack didn't get stopped right in its tracks. During the introduction of the performance, the school choir director, who is openly gay, mentioned that he was also the music director for that ministry. Once my niece got home, she called me completely distraught about what took place. This last year, God started allowing her to see things in the spirit and give her an understanding for spiritual warfare. As the youth director of our own church, I have always felt it is important for our youth to understand spiritual warfare and identify what is happening in the spirit. It is part of our youth curriculum to teach spiritual understanding. Our youth group studies have always been advanced, so her understanding of the spiritual realm is more in-depth than most teenagers. She shared her disappointment in her teacher for choosing a demonic song and especially because the event was being held in a church. This not only confused her but angered her. She kept saying she didn't understand why he would do that. This is an example of why you must be mindful of who you allow to have access over the people you are spiritually responsible for. I explained to her that the reason he thought it was okay to do a demonic song in a church is because he was already operating under a demonic hold. A demon will always seize an opportunity, especially within a church. I am not calling that director a demon, but the access that he gave the devil to his life, disqualified him from holding a position of leadership in a church, according to the Word of God. People must be able to trust their leaders the way that God trust's a pastor with his people.

Homosexuality was the gateway spirit, but no demonic spirit works alone. A gateway spirit is the spirit that holds the door open for all the other spirits that work hand in hand with it. For example, a spirit of depression is a gateway spirit to a suicide spirit. When you voluntarily allow a spirit to infiltrate your ministry, you give the devil access to it. That access allowed the choir director to be given an opportunity that brought secular music into a place that was sanctioned to reverence God. Though the pastors may not have known at first that the songs that would be sung would be a demonic type of ritual, the accountability remained theirs. The devil laid and waited for that church to compromise the guidelines set in scripture for leadership, to gain a position in the church. That compromise would later make room for an opportunity to sing and perform demonic rituals in the foyer of that church and attempt to speak curses over those that attended that school performance.

Once he was positioned just right, a request was made to use the church for the school event. This led to an open opportunity for the devil to cast a spell and open portals within the walls of the church, all while the pastors watched. As Christians and leaders, we must be bolder in the spirit of God, than demons are in the demonic realm. Making people uncomfortable is not a reason to allow the devil's attack to go uninterrupted. Christians choosing to be silent is still a decision made and not a good one. I pointed out to my niece another sign that this was an intentional act of the devil. Her last choir concert was at the school auditorium. They sang so many Christian songs at that concert that you would have thought they were a church choir. The next choir event was at the church, and this is when and where he thought it would be a good idea to sing the songs that was calling on spirits to open demonic portals. I later found out from my niece that the secular artist who sang this song did a video for it, with actual witches and warlocks doing a ritual.

It became evident that the cloaks and holding the microphones in that particular position, were an imitation of the real seance that was done in this music video. The devil knew exactly what he was doing, and he knew exactly where to do it at, because he had already broken into the ranks. The choir director was used to befriended the pastors and position himself. He wasn't stopped from joining the church choir and worked his way into being the choir director. If we just look at this spiritually, the pastors have given a demon the assignment to lead the people of God into an intimate place of worship meant to reverence the God that he despises. A spirit that God calls an abomination. Mind you, biblically this arrangement is not even spiritually possible. This is a prime example of how patient the devil will be to infiltrate your ministry by downplaying the condition of someone's spirit and their walk with God or lack of. Leaders who are not attentive or proactive, often will have bigger issues to clean up than those who have an effective preventive measure in place to protect the congregation and the integrity of the church early on. Even if they are anointed, if their heart posture and life is not in right standing with God, the spirit that they are operating in can be released over the church. When I am going through something, I know when I need to grab a set of worship flags and praise my way through some things. As a worshiper, instruments of worship are my choice of weapon against the enemy, along with prayer. When someone is going through, sometimes people must use their ministry to war through it. People who sing may need to sing through it, just like some people may shout or dance through their storm.

When should we remove them from participating in ministry? We must make sure that we leave room for grace and give them time to fight through it. Discernment from leadership and a careful eye will allow you to catch things before their problem becomes a church problem. If you are starting to see the shift in their posture or behavior, it may be time to suggest that they step away from the forefront. It may be best to allow them time to fight their battles behind closed doors. It is safe to allow people to still sing, dance or participate in ministry as they are battling things like depression, worry and trusting God and etc. This doesn't become a problem unless there starts to be spillage in the church or they are actively participating in sin. Example: Someone may be a prayer warrior but may be going through a tough time due to a spouse having an affair. They do not have to be set down because they have things going on; we all do at some point or another. When their prayers in front of the church start to consist of personal detailed information about the affair or stop glorifying God, they need some time to heal behind closed doors. If they are the one that is having the affair, they need to be set down immediately because they have chosen sin over godly living. Repentance and prayer is always going to be the best weapon to overcome a storm.

Leaders must stay observant, so they are aware when someone's flesh starts making cameo appearances in ministry. People who are going through can sometimes unknowingly release things over the church depending on their emotion, what they are going through and how they may be handling it. This may require there to be a slight correction for the sake of the ministry and spiritual health. Regardless of how that correction may be received, Proverbs 10:17 tells us that those who ignore correction will go astray.

## Proverbs 10:17 NLT

*"People who accept discipline are on the pathway to life, but those who ignore correction will go astray."*

When someone is operating in the wrong spirit or has a compromised spirit, it will only stay hidden for so long before it is exposed. When it has been hidden, God is giving grace and time to make it right. Unaddressed issues and hidden iniquities (sin) will be what will slowly fill their cup until it spills over. People think that the mess that is spilling over must resemble what they're dealing with but that's not always true. You can be guilty of stealing, lying or adultery and if you do not repent, your unwillingness to correct it can look like disrespect, offense, distractions, rebellion etc. These behaviors will continue to strengthen your flesh. These are just a few. A leader must use discernment to know when someone needs to be set down for a while. Though people can be set down for many reasons, being set down can often feel like punishment to those who don't quite get it. Sitting someone down from ministry is not about punishing them but is about protecting them and the people in the church. It is the job of the Shepherd and the leaders of the church to protect the congregation. Pastors need to keep in mind that God trusts them to fulfill their assignments and protect the souls of those assigned to them. If they allow these things to continue without intervening, they will give the enemy full access to the congregation. Uncorrected behavior is just a symptom of bigger issues and can cause a wave of negativity and division. It is better to prevent a spill than to have so many people sitting in the puddle. Regardless of whether someone is saved or not, the pastor should help guide you to building a healthy relationship with God, in truth and understanding. Though people may not receive everything that is said to them, they must understand that there should be constant growth and development, even when we are new to Christ. We must not be offended when leaders are correcting us as God has instructed them to do so. It is their job to prepare us for God's return. By giving us correction, we are being molded into the person God has created us to be. These corrections help prepare us to be accepted into the Kingdom of God. As we pursue our walk in Christ, we should take on the demeanor of Ephesians 4:14-15. This scripture should be a constant reminder of our spiritual goals and continued growth.

## Ephesians 4:14-15 NLT

*Then we will no longer be immature like children. We won't be tossed and blown about by every wind of new teaching. We will not be influenced when people try to trick us with lies so clever they sound like the truth. Instead, we will speak the truth in love, growing in every way more and more like Christ, who is the head of his body, the church.*

# Chapter 17

## Obedience vs. Manipulation

In a perfect world we could assume that every church leader or pastor will only lead their church by the unction of the Holy Spirit, but unfortunately this is not always the case. Though this should be the standard in running any church, the willingness to compromise the Word has left room for people to distort something that should be God based. Every Christian who is seeking God wholeheartedly knows being obedient to God's Word is vital to our walk with God.

When we join a church, we know that we must submit to the guidelines that the pastor has set for their church. There are people who will often claim manipulation or witchcraft because they do not want to line up with the directives set by the pastor. It is not manipulation or witchcraft because you were given guidelines, directives or instructions on how to do something. A key factor in telling the difference is being able to identify if the directive contradicts scripture. You want to be sure that what you perceive as manipulation is not just your unwillingness to be obedient or take direction. We must rely on the Word and not our feelings.

## Hebrews 13:17 NLT

*"Obey your spiritual leaders, and do what they say. Their work is to watch over your souls, and they are accountable to God. Give them reason to do this with joy and not with sorrow. That would certainly not be for your benefit.*

When does being obedient become a bad thing? There are so many scriptures that have been twisted to fit a particular narrative, but the

Bible speaks clearly about his Word being used as a weapon of manipulation.

## II Corinthians 4:2 NLT

*"We reject all shameful deeds and underhanded methods. We don't try to trick anyone or distort the word of God. We tell the truth before God, and all who are honest know this."*

What is manipulation? Let's talk about what it isn't. It is not of God. God doesn't operate in trickery, so manipulation is never a position in God's Kingdom or among God's people. Manipulation is an intentional or strategic act of deceit to convince or guilt someone to do something. Manipulation allows for someone to control another person or their behavior using tactics that will get them the outcome that the manipulator desires. People who manipulate are swindlers. God says there is no room for swindlers in the Kingdom of God.

## I Corinthians 6:9-10 ESV

*"Or do you not know that the unrighteous will not inherit the kingdom of God? Do not be deceived; neither the sexually immoral, nor idolaters, nor adulterers, nor men who practice homosexuality, nor thieves, nor the greedy, nor drunkards, nor revilers, nor swindlers will inherit the kingdom of God."*

So, what does manipulation look like in the church and when should you just say no? There is a variety of different types of manipulation in the church. These tactics are not biblical and can be subtle or more obvious than others. Manipulation may not always be recognized for what it is. Here are just a few of the most popular manipulation tactics used in churches.

## Commitment to the Church

This is where leaders have put members in a position to do work for the church without any consideration for a member's family. I have watched husbands angry at their wives and kids mad at their parents for spending more time at the church than with them. In an earlier chapter I said, "God's business, God's people and God's directives," so how could someone be wrong for taking care of church business?

# I Timothy 5:8 ESV

*"But if anyone does not provide for his relatives, and especially for members of his household, he has denied the faith and is worse than an unbeliever."*

That scripture explains if you do not take care of your own family, especially those in your own household, you have denied your faith. You cannot neglect your family and their needs and then say that you are a godly example. You cannot stand as a Christian without tending to the people that God has assigned to your household. Scripture says that you are worse than an unbeliever. Taking care of your family is still God's business. Though churches preach about putting your hands to work in the church, if you are neglecting your own home to do so, that is not the way to do it. You could cause a spouse to dislike the church or have a distorted vision of God because of how we manage our Christian journey. Let us be the example of great things and a reflection of God's goodness. This doesn't mean that you cannot work out something with your spouse. Let them know that there is a revival coming up next month. Make sure it is okay to order dinner those nights or make enough for leftovers so that you can attend. Taking care of your household is not just physical but impacts all areas of need. This may require spending extra time with your spouse before the revival or meal prepping for the kids. Try to make it as easy as possible for your family to adjust. Take care of the responsibilities in your home before committing to church business. I don't mean that you can't go to service because you didn't fold the clothes before you left, but attending church should help build your spiritual life and have a positive impact on your home. If the people in your home feel like they are competing with the church, there may be a lack of balance.

Church business never takes precedence over God's directive. What God says will always be the priority. Taking care of your family according to I Timothy 3:4-5, is one of the ways we show God that we are worthy of putting our hands to the plow in ministry. If you are unable to manage your own home and children in a manner worthy of full respect, how can you manage taking care of God's house?

## I Timothy 3:4-5 NLT

*"He must manage his own family well, having children who respect and obey him. For if a man cannot manage his own household, how can he take care of God's church?"*

## Fear

Fear of going to hell, the outcome or disappointing someone is another big manipulation tactic used. People in ministry can sometimes do things out of fear of disappointing others and other times it's self inflicted fear. I witnessed pastors tell members that if they don't do what they are told then will go to hell out of disobedience, even though the request isn't Christ-like. Instead of people speaking up, they do it out of fear of disappointing leadership or fear of being wrong if they refuse. The Bible is very specific in Matthew 10:28 on who we should fear.

## Matthew 10:28 ESV

*"And do not fear those who kill the body but cannot kill the soul. Rather fear him who can destroy both soul and body in hell."*

We should fear God not people. Our fear of God should not be a fear that reflects us being scared, but reverence. Reverence fear is like the fear we have for our parents. Despite their size, we respect them so much that we dare not cross them. This is the same type of fear we should have for God but 100 times more. Anyone who uses hell to guilt you into doing something for the church is trying to manipulate you. You must not do things that you have been manipulated into doing, especially if it does not line up with the Word of God. Take a moment to see what the Word says about the request being made if you have some hesitation. The Holy Spirit should have you questioning things that do not align with God. This can sometimes feel like a disruption in your spirit that makes you think this is not okay. If your spirit is aligned with God's and it's not right, there should be a hesitation in your spirit. Do not ignore the unction of the Holy Spirit, it's your helper. Do risk your place in the Book of Life because you were swindled into manipulating someone else. Having free will makes us accountable for our own actions before God.

## Financial Exploitation

Financial Exploitation is another tactic of manipulation. We should not be made to feel guilty or tricked into giving under compulsion. I have been in services that required all leaders in a church to give a certain amount during offering. Sometimes, God can lay it on the speaker's heart to do so but when it's God, there will be no need to hound, ridicule or hold the church hostage for the desired amount. As the giver, be sure that God is telling you to do so. The fact that everyone in the church can see who gives and who doesn't, can sometimes create an environment meant to apply pressure to the giver. This can indirectly cause embarrassment, which can lead to people giving even when they know they don't have it. If you are giving in faith, be sure there is an unction of the Holy Spirit confirming it. If God didn't tell you beforehand or there is no peace after it is mentioned, you should not give out of guilt, fear or shame. The Word says we shouldn't be reluctant or compulsive in our giving. Don't overthink it, your green light in these scenarios is the Holy Spirit. Some Christian organizations may operate with fees and dues but offerings are not to function the same way.

## II Corinthians 9:7 NLT

*"You must each decide in your heart how much to give. And don't give reluctantly or in response to pressure. 'For God loves a person who gives cheerfully."*

## Isolation (Ostracizing)

Isolation (Ostracizing) is another manipulation tactic that isn't of God. Over the years I have seen so many churches that have used isolation as a means of control. There are those that are isolated and those they are used for isolating. People must be careful that they don't become an avenue of control by being manipulated to mistreat, ignore, isolate or bully other Christians or people. There have been ministries that promote and encourage other members to turn their back or unfriend people who have chosen to leave the church. I have heard so many leaders that have said if you leave their church that you will miss your blessing because God will not know where to find you or that God won't have an address for you. It's one of those terms that make me cringe every time I hear it come across the pulpit. Let me clear up the misconception that has been presented as truth without any real context. Whether you leave or stay in a ministry has nothing to do with God locating you. God should always find you in a posture of willingness to be obedient and to hear him. God is an omnipresent God, which means that God is everywhere at all times. Your physical location has no relevance to God's reach, though he should be able to find you in the same location all the time, in his will and not outside of it.

## Psalm 139:7-12 NIV

*Where can I go from your Spirit? Where can I flee from your presence? If I go up to the heavens, you are there; if I make my bed in the depths, you are there. If I rise on the wings of the dawn, if I settle on the far side of the sea, even there your hand will guide me, your right hand will hold me fast. If I say, "Surely the darkness will hide me and the light become night around me," even the darkness will not be dark to you; the night will shine like the day, for darkness is as light to you."*

Those are just a few of the common tactics that people have used to scare members into staying in their ministry. Remind yourself that God does not work in fear, so anything meant to provoke fear is not of God. The phrase that God won't be able to find you is a contradiction of the capabilities of God. This is why we must know what the Word says for ourselves. Should we say no to leadership when their request conflicts with our spirit? Anything that contradicts God's character is not of God, regardless of who the messenger is. We acknowledge that certain people are chosen to lead, teach and pastor God's people, but we must stand firm on biblical principles, rather than following people who misuse their titles to justify ungodly behavior and demands in His name. We must be accountable for our own decisions and actions. Blaming someone else for our behavior doesn't remove the accountability. If representing someone causes you to misrepresent Christ, you should boldly refuse. When approached with this type of despicable opportunity, Galatians 1:10 is a great scripture to stand on.

## Galatians 1:10 ESV

*"For am I now seeking the approval of man, or of God? Or am I trying to please man? If I were still trying to please man, I would not be a servant of Christ."*

## Peer Pressure

Peer pressure is another tactic. Though this can be a tough one to get through, peer pressure is not a permission slip to be ungodly. There is an accountability that must be met that has nothing to do with leadership or those that are leading. Just like the actions of our leaders don't gain us any points in our walk with God, our actions because of our leaders don't excuse us from it either. To be a vessel for God, we cannot be a vessel for man and Acts 5:29 makes that clear.

## Acts 5:29 ESV

*"But Peter and the apostles answered, 'We must obey God rather than men.'"*

We must have integrity within our own salvation to not be snared into a behavior that the enemy is spearheading in the background.

## Proverbs 11:3 ESV

*"The integrity of the upright guides them, but the crookedness of the treacherous destroys them."*

The Word of God tells us to use wisdom in our decisions. Sometimes we must declare scripture to stand on God's Word. In that moment, declare Psalm 25:21.

# Psalm 25:21 ESV

*"May integrity and uprightness preserve me, for I wait for you."*

# Chapter 18

## Money vs. Offering

I have heard so many people throughout the years, even before my salvation, who have complained about giving an offering to the church and where it was going. I have heard everything from, "I am not paying the Pastor to drive around in a Mercedes," to "I am not paying for the Pastor's mortgage."

People will complain about the $1 they put in the basket for tithes or offering but if a $1 is what God laid on your heart to put in the basket, there should be no conditions tied to it. If your heart is troubled about your offering or your tithes, regardless of the amount, do not put it in the basket. God see's your heart before the church see's your money. If you cannot give it with a loving heart, without malice, anger, accusations and distaste, you minus well keep it. Many people do not understand there is a difference between giving *your* money and giving an offering.

An offering is an act of worship, obedience to God and gratitude. It is the way the Bible says we symbolically give God back what is rightfully his. When we give an offering, we tell God that all we have belongs to him, and we rely fully on him to take care of us. It is easy to start to feel like we are the ones making it possible to pay our bills. How many times have we looked up and noticed that we just got paid and it looks like our bank accounts are nearly empty? Naturally, worry and panic start to set in on what to do to make ends meet. However, when we rely on God and give our offering, we tell God, this little bit will not make me or break me, because you will do more for me than any amount that I could ever give you in return. We know that we could never give God all that he deserves. We couldn't even get close but our offering is not about the church or a means of payment. It's an act of reverence. Our mindset should be, "God gave me this job, this car, and this home, so this check belongs to him."

So, what's the difference between *your* money and offering? Your heart posture. Your heart posture determines whether what you put in the basket is *your* money or an offering. An offering is to God, an acknowledgment, worship, and reverence. When you give an offering, it is about God. When you are giving *your* money, it will often come with stipulations or emotional attachments. An example of this is when someone drops fifty dollars into the offering basket, but they have reservations because there is a condition in which they believe their money should be used. Giving *their* money can also cause them to speak poorly of a ministry or the leaders, because of the known or unknown use of the money. When someone gives *their* money, not only does it come with a stipulation or emotional attachment, their actions often reflect the behavior of someone with a tainted or wounded heart. There is no way to give an offering and stake claims to it after you have given it to God.

When giving an offering, the moment it is dropped into the basket, it is given with an understanding that this is not about anyone else but God. Who God has appointed over the house, is who he trusts to manage all things concerning his house. You must trust God more than you distrust others. This goes back to trusting your leadership. Do not curse yourself by cursing or speaking poorly of the Man or Woman of God because of your insecurities. An offering belonging to God has no personal claim to it. Can you imagine putting money in the basket and then telling God, well I am only giving this to you if you use it for what I say? Imagine being okay with the pastor using the money for a new pulpit to be built but you become resentful if it's used for the children's church. What boldness and pride must we possess to take this posture. Isn't all that is in God's house governed by who God has appointed to manage and run it? There are churches that give options on the church envelopes to choose certain ministries to apply your offering to. It's okay to do so when the shepherd of the house has opened the door for this to be annotated. The problem is not in the assignment of the money but of the heart, reaction and expectation in which someone has given it. If the pastor decided that until they meet a certain amount for the children's church all proceeds will be applied to the children's church, this shouldn't cause anger to the giver. It's all given to support the vision God has for that house. When giving an offering at a church that may not offer a choice to designate it, do not speak negative words or opinions based on your own conclusions or assumptions. If God has already given you a directive to give to a certain ministry, be obedient, but remember God see's your heart before he sees your offering. Don't lie on God to push your own agenda. This should be done with a loving and cheerful heart and not with expectations,malice, anger, bitterness, aggravation, or any other emotion that the enemy can hitchhike his agenda to. Use your tongue to speak life with affirmations and declarations, instead of death with verbal curses and accusations. Remember you are to be obedient to Christ. If the pastor uses the money in an area that differs from what you agree with, you should honor the pastor's directive. Leave the responsibility of obedience between him and God. Do not make God's servant your enemy because of your feelings.

## Proverbs 18:21 KJV

*"Death and life are in the power of the tongue and they that love it shall eat the fruit thereof."*

## Exodus 20:16 MSG

*"No lies about your neighbor."*

It is better for you not to give *your* money than to give with a tainted heart. If giving is going to cause you to be angry or bitter before or after you give, you should not waste your time or money. God does not want *your* money, he wants you to give what is rightfully his, but he only wants it if it given with a cheerful heart.

You should now have a clear understanding of the difference between giving an offering and giving your money. Offerings belong to God. It is God's possession, in our care, given in reverence and worship without an emotional attachment, preference or stipulation (condition). Your money is money in your possession, given to God from your pocket and not your heart. It comes with emotional attachments and preferences.

1. What is the difference between your offering and your money?

   _____

   _____

   _____

2. Should you withhold from giving if you feel the pastor is not properly using the money? Why or why not?

   _____

   _____

   _____

3. Which comes with stipulations, your offering or your money?

   _____

   _____

   _____

   _____

# Chapter 19

## Is Tithing a Requirement?

Tithing is one of those subjects that has divided people in the Christian community and unbelievers alike because of lack of understanding. Does the Bible say that we must tithe, what is a tithe and where in the Bible does it specify how much we are to give? Well, the answer is an all in one.

## Malachi 3:10 NLT

*"Bring all the tithes into the storehouse so there will be enough food in my Temple. If you do," says the Lord of Heaven's Armies, "I will open the windows of heaven for you. I will pour out a blessing so great you won't have enough room to take it in! Try it! Put me to the test!"*

Malachi 3:10 specifically tells us to bring our tithes to the church, so that there will be enough food in God's temple. In this scripture, it is not just referring to physical and edible food. The food in this scripture is the need of the church. In current times, the need would be mortgage or rent, electricity, water and anything else that the church may have a need for. This includes what is needed for ministry. This scripture not only answers if we should tithe to the church, but why should we tithe to the church. The scripture continues to tell us what our reward is for giving our tithes. God says, I will pour out a blessing so great you will not have enough room to take it in. This is a scripture that I can say has proven to be true, time and time again. I used to not be a tither. I would hear repeatedly that if you give your tithes, God will provide for you. I heard all the stories stories to put God first and he'll take care of you, and I believed it in my heart but not in my mind. I believed that God was fully capable of everything everyone said. I never really thought about my thought process until I started giving tithes consistently. Even as a Christian, I was not giving consistently. I could not figure out how I could afford to tithe. If you feel the same way, then you are where I used to be and do not have a true understanding of what it means to tithe. I knew God could do all that his Word said, but I did not trust God to do it for me. At first, I didn't know why I felt that way but I realized that I didn't feel like I was holy enough for God to do for me what he did for those who were further along in their relationship with God than myself. I realized I was following someone I did not trust. I knew God to be trustworthy and I trusted him for everyone else, but I did not trust him for myself. How was that even possible? My thought process could not have been further from the truth. What God said about tithing had nothing to do with position or level of salvation.

One day I decided I was going to start giving my tithes consistently. Most people who have this same mindset can't wrap their mind around giving their tithes when it feels like they are barely scraping by. First thing is to open your eyes to the truth. Our tithes are given to God but the address it is delivered to is his church. This is no different than you mailing a payment back to a company when they have overpaid you. Deciding to keep what is rightfully theirs because you do not like the address is still keeping something that is not yours. God gives us all that we have and then tells us to give ten percent of what he gives us to his house (church) to take care of his family (congregation). Think about how God must see us when we don't give God what's his. What if someone kept what was needed for your household? The key to all of this is God provides everything we have, including opportunities, employment, promotions and even things given. Do not discredit God's goodness because of how big or small the blessing is.

Tithes and faith both work together. Faith requires us to believe God for somethings that we cannot see. This includes things we cannot understand and trusting God when we do not know how God is going to do something. The "how" is never our business. If you could have fixed it by yourself, you would have. You cannot trust God and still be in his way. You become God's obstacle. We all know that God could handle anything thrown in his direction, but because God gives us free will, our decisions could turn God away. We are the only ones that can tie God's hands in our own lives. Fear of tithing can cause us to miss out on some of the great things that God wants to do for us. I took the end of Malachi 3:10 to heart, when God said try it and put him to the test. As sure as I am that there is a God, I became a consistent tither and seen God do just what he said. When I started tithing, I expected that God was going to increase my bank account with unknown amounts of money, unexpected checks or people would just voluntarily give me money like the testimonials on television. Though all those things are possible, that was not my experience. However, God still kept his Word. I want to make sure that no one misses this, especially if you have struggled with tithing or being consistent.

In I Kings 17:8-15, God tells the Prophet, Elijah to go live in a city called Zarephath, where he has instructed a widow there to feed him. Once Elijah went to the city and met the widow, he asked the lady for a cup of water and some bread. The widow informed him that she had no bread made and that she was about to prepare the last of it for her and her son. She explained this would be their last meal before they would die. The crops were not manifesting and there had been no rain. Elijah told her to make him some bread first and then continue to make a meal for her and her son. He then spoke what he heard God say. "There will always be flour and olive oil left in the containers until the time when the Lord sends rain and the crops grow again." When she did what Elijah said, there was always enough flour and olive oil left in the containers, just as the Lord had promised. This allowed food for her son and herself until there were crops. Well, this was my experience with my tithes. I did not get enormous amounts of money delivered to my bank account. What I experienced is exactly what the widow experienced when she was obedient to the directions given by Elijah. I realized that though I did not see an increase in dollar amounts in my account, I often paid my bills after my tithes and would acknowledge that the amount left was not as much as I would have liked. As the weeks went by, I could not make sense of how I kept buying things I needed, and I still had more money left than I expected. I had no need for anything. I was shocked. The next month, the same thing happened and then the month after that. My money seemed to increase in volume and not in dividends. I started realizing I had more money left over at the end of the month than I would before I started tithing. Again, I was shocked. I became a faithful tither with consistent results of God keeping his word. I gave my tithes, and every time God took care of all my needs but on paper, none of it made sense. It looked impossible. The significance of that was in the presentation of the word, I-m-possible (I am possible). I know for a fact that God keeps his Word. Before this final revelation there were other factors that played heavily into my misdirected understanding.

I used to ask my mother, who is an evangelist in the church, "Mom, how do you give your tithes when it is all you have?" She said, "You have to trust God." She was right, you do, but it was not until I was writing this chapter that God revealed to me a big piece of my problem. I was making the same mistake that most people make, and it was right there in Deuteronomy.

## Deuteronomy 26:2 NLT

*"...put some of the first produce from each crop you harvest into a basket and bring it to the designated place of worship-the place the Lord your God chooses for his name to be honored..."*

So, what was the mistake I was making? I was not giving God the first of anything. I was scared and would panic because I was paying my bills and then looking at the remainder of what was left. I kept questioning how I was going to make it the rest of the month if I paid tithes. I felt like I wanted to do more for God but I couldn't afford to. I felt like if I could, I would, but I couldn't. I felt helpless. This allowed the enemy to wreak havoc in my mind. I was not giving God what was his. The first of what we have belongs to God and then God allows us to keep the rest; but fear had me struggling to be obedient to God's directive. Many people who don't experience the outcome God has expressed in Malachi, has a visa-versa approach to the foundation of tithing. We always want to have the heart to give our last, but we never want our last to be the first thing we give to God. People may believe that giving God their last is coming from a place of sacrifice, but denying God what is his first to give God what is our last is nothing more than giving God the crumbs at his own table. We should not position ourselves to give God what remains. Leave your crumbs for the birds to pick through, not God. No matter how important we think our last may be to us, it is dishonorable to think that God deserves what we deem important, instead of what God tells us is important.

## Proverbs 3:9-10 NLT

*"Honor the Lord with your wealth and with the best part of everything you produce. Then he will fill your barns with grain, and your vats will overflow with good wine."*

When we give our God our best, God will then in turn take care of our needs. We cannot follow God's directive in part and expect to reap what the Bible says we are supposed to. The word "tithe" derives from the old English word "teogotha," which means tenth. God will honor his Word, but will you be obedient to reap the reward? If you choose not to follow God's directive, then you cannot reap the benefits of tithing, but will experience the consequences of your disobedience. I use to think, "they don't know what I have going on," but God does.? There is also a scripture that speaks of those who don't have an income to tithe from.

## II Corinthians 8:12 AMP

*For if the eagerness (to give) is there, it is acceptable according to what a person has, not according to what he does not have.*

This scripture tells us that God honors the heart of the giver. Tithing is a posture of the heart and should not be determined by if you think you can spare it. You want to know if you have it or not? My father, Bishop Dietrich Butcher, summed it up sitting on the living room couch better than anyone I ever heard across the pulpit. He said, "tithing is sacrificing from a place of need." I could have just wrote that one sentence and ended the chapter right there. That said it all. If you don't think you need it then God don't want it. It's not tithing if it doesn't require faith and sacrifice. One of my mistake was trying to fit my tithes into my budget the way I factored in my bills every month. So how do you know if you have it to give? When you get paid do you have ten percent? Then your tithes is there because it is the first of what you receive.

Tithes are based on a few things, your heart posture, your sacrifice and what you have been given, not what you can give. If you pay bills and then look for your tithes, you will never find it because your tithes was the first part of your check. If you have failed to see the benefits of tithing, go back to his Word and figure out where you may have cut corners in his instructions. Sometimes our anger can be misdirected at God, when it is our own actions that keep us from seeing the benefits of our obedience. If you missed it, read the instructions again and go from there.

## *Isaiah 55:11 NLT*

*"It is the same with my word. I send it out, and it always produces fruit. It will accomplish all I want it to, and it will prosper everywhere I send it."*

There was one more thing that held me hostage from paying tithes. You may have noticed there are parts in this chapter that say pay tithes and other parts that say give tithes. Where you see the phrase pay tithes, it expresses my mindset at the time that I was trying to process what it meant to tithe. It was a mindset that I didn't even realize I had until it was revealed in my writing. Understanding the difference positioned my heart closer to God. We do not "pay" our tithes, we "give" our tithes. We cannot even begin to give God all that he deserves. This is why God doesn't ask us to pay tithes, but to give them. There is no valid reason that we cannot give to God what is his, though there are excuses to try to justify not tithing.

There is a saying if you want to see what's important to someone, look at their bank account. Is God's portion taken from the beginning or the end of your account? You may need to make an adjustment. Tithing allows us to promote a spirit of generosity and keeps us relying on God instead of ourselves. Tithing is necessary to stay naturally accountable for our spiritual dependency. It is a constant reminder that despite what we have, we trust and depend on God for all things needed.

Check in:

1. Name something that you read that stood out to you while reading?_____

_____

_____

_____

2. Who does a Five-Fold Ministry consist of?_____

_____

_____

_____

_____

3. What are the 3 Rules of Never?_____

_____

_____

_____

_____

_____

_____

_____

4. What is the misconception of being set down and what's the truth?

_____

_____

_____

_____

_____

_____

5. What are the 3 C's?

_____

_____

_____

_____

_____

## Chapter 20

## *Choosing Between Offering or Tithes*

Is it possible to give tithes instead of offering and still Honor God, or the other way around? This is such a common question, but no one wants to ask the question out loud.

## Malachi 3:8-10 NLT

*"Should people cheat God? Yet you have cheated me! "But you ask, 'What do you mean? When did we ever cheat you?'" "You have cheated me of the tithes and offerings due to me..."*

I used to believe that I knew everything I needed to know about tithing and offering based on what I heard my whole entire life. I had no idea of the depth of what tithing and offering meant or consisted of until I read it for myself. There was so much more to it than dropping money for a building fund and parting ways with some of my income. I have read things about offering and tithes in the Bible that I have never heard come across the pulpit or seen in all the years I have been saved. God has truly opened my eyes and has now given me an avenue to share this with the world. I use to believe that an offering was a little extra money that people blessed the church with. Malachi 3:8-10 makes it crystal clear, that one without the other is still stealing from God. I know it would sound better to say, "you did not give God what is rightfully his," but this book should be building your understanding and spiritual maturity as you read it. I can't afford to give you all the sweet stuff without giving you all the sour. That price is too high to pay.

These are principles of truth that can change our lives drastically for the good or the bad. We often get caught up in the niceties of the Word of God and miss or skim over the things that may be a little harder to swallow. It is the things that are harder to swallow that we should be reading with a magnifying glass. We do not want to ignore the things we are accountable for, just to be comfortable temporarily. Being temporarily comfortable can cause us to be eternally uncomfortable. The consequence is too great to water down the truth. So, in black in white, no we cannot give one without giving the other because both belong to God.

Read Malachi 3 for a deeper understanding.

# Chapter 21

## Should Pastors Receive a Salary

Sometimes, I wish pastors would put the electric bill up for the month so people could see how their $20 for the year barely cover the snacks their kids eat in children's church. Though the posture of your heart can position that $20 to multiply 200 times more out of obedience, people tend to give money more weight than what is correct. If you hold a position on your job, you manage everything that comes with that position. However, even if you love your job, you deserve compensation for your time and commitment. Pastor's work for the biggest boss of them all, God. God does not expect his followers to fend for themselves. People expect pastors to answer their phone call day or night, pray and war for them, pay for electric, water, lights, rent or mortgage for the church out of their own pockets, all while maintaining their own households. That is not to include the expectation not to vacation, so they are always available. On paper, it is not even a reasonable request, though in people's minds they question why should a church pay a pastor a salary? The question is easy to answer.

As the church grows, so does the demand physically, spiritually, and naturally, including the bills. Should we bless our Pastors for selflessly doing God's work? Why wouldn't we want to bless the person that God has sent to lead, teach and cover us? I could go into a debate about all the pastors and leaders who have been accused for using church funds for airplanes and things, but the truth is, I don't know what God told them. What I do know is that with every position, every decision and every assignment there must be a clear direction from God. I cannot tell you what God did or did not say to those other pastors, but we should always tread carefully on who and what we speak on. Regardless of if they have done something wrong in that moment, we also may not understand or have privy to everything that comes along with a pastor's decision. For example, someone heard that the pastor brought a ten bedroom ranch, and everyone's head turned but no one knows how he purchased it.

People start assuming and the chatter starts. No one knows that God told him to buy that ranch because he would be starting a teen mentor program, where runaway youth would get a second chance. They would be housed, loved, and taught the Word of God. No one knows that he had to give up his own private home for collateral for the down payment. No one knows he fasted and prayed with his own family for months for God to tell him what to do. No one knows his family would no longer have the privacy they once had because they must live among these teens until the program takes off. No one ever thinks of the sacrifices that pastors must make in their personal lives to be obedient in their spiritual walk. No one considers that the pastor and his family cannot even think about purchasing another private home until this assignment is successful and they can afford to pay staff. Obedience to God doesn't always come with cheerleaders and support. Sometimes obedience can leave you in a place of solitude. If you need to know all the details to trust your pastor, then you are under the wrong leadership or you have allowed the enemy too much headway. Church isn't just a building of people wanting to serve God and collect money. This goes back to choosing your house. Can you trust your leaders?

Though you may want to know the ins and outs of everything that goes on in the church, that will never be the case. How money is being spent in the church will always be an open opportunity for the devil to cause waves for the Kingdom. Though the pastors and leaders should carry the character that the Word has described, we have seen pastors fall short and become caught up in some type of scandal. We must pray that those pastors realign themselves or God clears their name. The inability to do so usually results in exposure.

Though there have been more than one or two who have been exposed, there are more pastors with good standing than bad. We must not make permanent decisions, spiritually or naturally because of those who have fallen. If this was a different scenario, would you make the decision not to put your money in the bank anymore, because it was robbed? Just as the money in the bank is insured to protect the people, God is our insurance. Once we give it to God, if it is misappropriated, we do not have to concern ourselves with it because God insures any offering given from the heart of a giver. Never allow someone else's action to dictate the posture of your heart. It is good practice to apply your concept to different scenarios and see if it still makes sense. This will allow you to identify if your decision is based on your feelings instead of wise judgment.

Pastors have a physical accountability to their church and to God. We must trust that the accountability to God comes with enough conviction that their accountability to the church is handled correctly. Those that have found themselves in legal trouble for purchases outside of the legal scope of the church, have failed to maintain the requirements by God. In good conscious, those pastors should be held accountable. Each church should have their own by-laws created by the pastor, that explain how they will handle different decisions and financial spending. The church is built on the vision that God has given them. The by-laws are built on how God has instructed the pastor to run the church, which aligns with the vision. It is not likely that the same two churches will have the same exact vision or by-laws, because every assignment on the house (church) is different. This is where the standard for the functioning of the church is determined. Like ministry, the vision and the by-laws should also align with the Word of God. Though people may not like every decision, this is not up to the congregation. Regardless of what people may feel, the vision given to the pastor, including the by-laws, is not a congregational decision.

As men and women of God, we are supposed to be the example of Godly living. No one is perfect but if you are not attempting to correct things that go against the vision or the by-laws, you are headed down a path that gives the enemy room to cause discord. The Word tells us not to let our good be spoken evil of. This isn't about someone questioning your integrity, it's about ensuring that we are not the reason people question the integrity of the House of God. We may not do things to appease people, but we must be sure that we handle God's house in a way that is honorable and respectable. The House of God should also have a reputation that is respected in and out of the church. With that being said, the church must follow the proper protocol to ensure that things are done accordingly. Pastor's that will not follow the directive that God gave them for their church's finances and order, leave the door wide open for the enemy to tempt and damage the reputation of the church and themselves. This can cause distrust within the House of God. When financial decisions are made correctly, there is no room for conclusions. Rumors can easily be shut down without any scandal. Precautions are usually in place, but nothing can be guaranteed. Behavior should not be what you base your decision on. Your decisions should reflect the directions that have been given to us through the Word.

There is so much to do in the Kingdom of God and pastors have a big responsibility. Should there be a salary for those in the Kingdom? Ministry can be a full-time job and is usually more demanding because of the spiritual aspect but wisdom should be used when making decisions regarding God's business. If the church has broken windows that need to be repaired, the maintenance of God's house should be a address.

## Galatians 6:6 NLT

*"Those who are taught the word of God should provide for their teachers, sharing all good things with them."provide for their teachers, sharing all good things with them."*

An easy gauge of when it is okay, when it is not, and when it is the correct timing is to remember one simple rule. God first. Which means, God's directive, God's house, and God's people. No matter what someone else may have done in their church, people must listen carefully to what God is saying specifically about their own church. His directive will always outweigh what others think should happen. What if God relied on you to make sure that his chosen vessel is being taken care of? What if your ministry was the one God appointed to take care of his servant, the same way God told Elijah he directed a woman to feed him once he reached Zarephath? There are people that feel like there is no way that a pastor should get a salary. You have the right to express your opinion but let me put things into perspective.

Can you imagine a pastor trying to council all those people who need it, oversee the different ministries and still try to ensure that he is personal and not just a figment on the pulpit? Full time ministry is not for everyone, but it isn't something that we should tell people they do not have a right to do. It is like a stay-at-home mom. Some people feel like they should be home with their kids and others feel like they should be working. Meanwhile, others think they should only stay home the first few months and others think, "absolutely not." To each their own. In Corinthians 9, Paul spoke of how he refused a salary for doing God's work at the conviction of his own heart. He didn't want to give anyone any room to accuse him of something that is not true. He says that because of his work for the Lord, God has given him the right to reap from those he spiritually serves. Which in count means, those God has called to pastor, have a right to benefit from all they have done in ministry.

You must understand that God gives us the right to receive the benefits of ministry without guilt. People who have no full understanding of God's intention, will sometimes turn their nose up at someone who receives money from a ministry. It is important to not let someone else guilt you for accepting what God says is rightfully yours.

There are some stories or scenarios where leaders may have gained financially in a way that is not conducive with the intentions of God. I am not here to explain their actions. That is between them and God. I am here to explain what God expects from us and how we should manage Kingdom business. God see's all and knows all. He does not need you to investigate his people's spiritual shortcomings. This type of pursuit can build a bias in your heart against God's people, unknowingly. God needs you to be in prayer. Though Paul had refused his right to reap the benefits of his work in ministry, it does not mean others have to make the same decision. A pastor deciding to accept a salary offered to him, does not take him out of the will of God. It is merely him, accepting what God has said is rightfully his to receive.

## I Corinthians 9:7 NLT

*"What soldier has to pay his own expenses? What farmer plants a vineyard and does not have the right to eat some of its fruit? What shepherd cares for a flock of sheep and isn't allowed to drink some of the milk?"*

## I Corinthians 9:13-14 NLT

*"Do you not realize that those who work in the temple get their meals from the offerings brought to the temple? And those who serve at the altar get a share of the sacrificial offerings. In the same way, the Lord ordered that those who preach the Good News should be supported by those who benefit from it."*

So, should we give pastors a salary? The answer is, by the authority of God, it is their God given right to receive one

For a deeper understanding of Paul's heart, read I Corinthians 9.

# Chapter 22

## Restoring Honor to the House Of God

There have been so many excuses, plots, ploys, and promotional tactics to attract the world to the church. The same antics used to entice the world to come to church are the same type of antics that will be needed to keep them comfortable enough to stay. Leaders have started playing worldly music in the church, in the parking lot, cursing in the pulpits, opening the pulpit to secular music artists to sing, dance, pray and worship with no true spiritual relationship with God. This is more problematic for those attending and the souls that are being sacrificed for popularity and membership. This is a distinct sign of there being trouble in the house. The assignment given by God has been distorted with the desire to gain members for the church instead of souls for the Kingdom. God does not need a gimmick or a promotional tactic to draw people to salvation. If they are willing to look like, talk like and behave like the world, it is impossible for them to look like, talk like and behave like God at the same time.

We should resemble Christ in all we do; representing him in a way that doesn't have people wondering if we are one of God's children. What you do for the Kingdom should not causes you to compromise the integrity of the Holy Spirit. What do I mean? There should be no reason that you are giving spiritual correction, but your demeanor doesn't resemble Christ-like behavior. Our personal goal should be to handle each person as a soul for the Kingdom of God. Ask yourself, "is my behavior something I proudly want to have to answer to God for?"

# II Timothy 4:2-3 ESV

*Preach the word: be ready in season, out of season; reprove, rebuke, & exhort w/ complete patience & teaching. For the time is coming when people will not endure sound teaching, but having itching ears that will accumulate for themselves teachers to suit their own passion and will turn away from listening to the truth and wander off into myths.*

Scripture tells us that in our obedience to II Timothy 4:2-3, God will see us as a vessel that has been properly prepared for his use. This does not mean that we will not make mistakes or ever fall. However, the moment we ask God to forgive us of our sins, our sin is remembered no longer. We are to be set apart and to be set apart is to not look like the world in their sin. We are to be remnants of the Kingdom.

Remnants are God's faithful and chosen people preserved by God

# II Timothy 2:21 ESV

*"Therefore, if anyone cleanses himself from what is dishonorable, he will be a vessel for honorable use, set apart as holy, useful to the master of the house, ready for every good work."*

Why is it that so many churches have started to compromise what the Word says, for what the world says? Christians who know that these tactics and antics are not of God but have accepted this mockery of Christ, will also be judged. Participating in someone else's sin also has it's place in judgment. Once you partake in someone else's sin, it also becomes yours. You will also have to account for your actions.

I remember quite some years back; I was living as a sinner with Christian intentions. I had a friend who suffered a great emotional trauma at the hands of her husband. One day she said she had something to tell me. I asked casually, "Are you about to tell me you are gay?" I did not have to guess. I knew in my spirit that the enemy had finagled his way through that trauma door and set her up to be his victim. At this point in my life, I was not saved but we slowly became distant. She no longer felt as comfortable around me and over time we went our separate ways; checking in on each other every so many years. Eventually, I went on to get saved and she continued living the life she chose or the life the enemy chose for her. It really depends on how you want to look at it. Though being saved was not a new thing for me, my spiritual growth closely reflected one of a new Christian. Years later, she randomly asked me if she got married would I be one of her bridesmaids. I politely declined and told her that I could not be a part of a ceremony that I do not agree with. I re-iterated that I am a preacher's kid and that I do not believe in same sex marriage.

I was doing my best to live a godly life though I was not sure how to properly pursue God. Spiritually, I was still a babe in Christ, but God allowed me to discern accurately what I was feeling in the spirit. I remember her tearing up and telling me I was going to make her cry, but I stood my ground. I explained my spiritual stand and even told her I could do her bouquets if she wanted but I just could not participate in the ceremony. If I knew then, what I know now. I grew up in a Christian household and believe it or not, I had never seen this scripture until I started this book. I always thought I could go and support her as a friend and just help her set up. This is when being humble and always willing to learn has its advantages. We should never be so sure of ourselves that we are ashamed to admit what we don't know. In my head, I believed if I did not participate in the ceremony then there would be no blood (sin) on my hands. Boy, I could not have been further from the truth.

## I Timothy 5:22 KJV

*"Lay hands suddenly on no man, neither be partaker of other men's sins: keep thyself pure."*

I did not understand that it did not matter how small the part was; any act of participation compromised my salvation. Regardless of how little I participated, anything I contributed to her event was going to be used to partake in something that was made to mock the covenant God intended for man and woman. This was one of the biggest eye- awakening moments. While I found no sin in making a bridal bouquet or decorating, I failed to realize that the sin was not in what I made, but what it was going to be used for. My willingness to compromise to console her almost made me accountable for something that I was trying to avoid altogether. Compromising the Word of God by accepting the antics of the enemy will never work in our favor. We should guard ourselves from interactions, events and behaviors that cause us to engage in things that are not of God.

## James 2:10 KJV

*"For whosoever shall keep the whole law, and yet offend in one point, he is guilty of all."*

# CLOSING DECLARATION

I am God fearing.
I am not perfect, but I am a willing vessel.
I am accountable for my walk in Christ,
and I will not let anyone determine how I will talk or treat people.

I am a Man/Woman of God with spiritual integrity.
I will honor who God has positioned to lead me.
I will support the ministry that I have been
assigned to.
I will give, not just my heart,
but my tithes and offering to God
because I owe God everything.

My character will produce a behavior that resembles God's love,
His heart of forgiveness and his grace.
I will use wisdom in my decisions to honor God.
I will worship and praise him because I acknowledge who he is.

The relationship I have with him in front and behind closed
doors will resemble each other in truth.
For this is just the beginning of a new understanding.
I am strengthening my foundation,
For my next level.
I am a willing vessel for his Kingdom and his Glory.

May God's Will Be Done.

www.ingramcontent.com/pod-product-compliance
Lightning Source LLC
Chambersburg PA
CBHW060413090426
42734CB00011B/2304